A Fiery Heart

Lay Fraternities of St Dominic
At Sacred Heart Church
Bath PA 18014
St Louis de Montfort
Chapter #406

A Fiery Heart

THE RADICAL LOVE OF SAINT FRANCIS OF ASSISI

Felice Accrocca

Translated by Damian Bacich, Ph.D.

Our Sunday Visitor
Huntington, Indiana

Copyright © 2020 — Libreria Editrice Vaticana
Vatican City

The chapters in this book were originally published as articles in *L'Osservatore Romano*. The author has organized them here according to the timeline of Saint Francis's life.

25 24 23 22 21 20   1 2 3 4 5 6 7 8 9

All rights reserved. With the exception of short excerpts for critical reviews, no part of this work may be reproduced or transmitted in any form or by any means whatsoever without permission from the publisher.

For more information, visit www.osv.com/permissions.

Published in English by Our Sunday Visitor Publishing Division, Our Sunday Visitor Inc., 200 Noll Plaza, Huntington, IN 46750; 1-800-348-2440; www.osv.com.

ISBN: 978-1-68192-621-6 (Inventory No. T2484)
1. RELIGION—Christianity—Saints & Sainthood.
2. BIOGRAPHY & AUTOBIOGRAPHY—Religious.
3. RELIGION—Christianity—Catholic.

eISBN: 978-1-68192-622-3
LCCN: 2020950494

Cover design: Amanda Falk
Cover art: Crosiers
Interior design: Amanda Falk

PRINTED IN THE UNITED STATES OF AMERICA

Abbreviations

The following abbreviations are used to refer to early sources by and about Saint Francis and Saint Clare. With each citation, we have included the reference to the Italian version contained in *Fonti Franciscane*, the most complete collection of early Franciscan texts available.

    FF   *Fonti Franciscane*. Edited by E. Caroli, Padua 2011.

WRITINGS OF FRANCIS OF ASSISI

Adm	Admonitions
Cant	The Canticle of Brother Sun
2Lf	Letter to the Faithful II
Lmin	Letter to Minister
LOrd	Letter to the Entire Order
Rb	Regula Bullata (Later Rule)
Rnb	Regula Non Bullata (Early Rule)
Test	Testament of Saint Francis

HAGIOGRAPHIES OF SAINT FRANCIS OF ASSISI

Anper	Witness of the Anonymous of Perugia
CAs	Assisi Compilation
1Cel	Thomas of Celano, First *Life of Saint Francis* [*Vita prima*]
2Cel	Thomas of Celano, Second *Life of Saint Francis* or *Memoriale* [*Vita seconda*]
3Comp	The Legend of the Three Companions
Flo	The Little Flowers of Saint Francis
LegM	Bonaventure of Bagnoregio, *Legenda Major*

CHRONICLES AND OTHER TESTIMONIES

Eccleston   Thomas of Eccleston, *The Friars and How They Came to England* (De Adventu F.F. Minorum in Angliam)
Jordan   Jordan of Giano, *Chronicle*
2Vitry   Jacques de Vitry *Letter VI* (1220) from Damietta
VitryHoc   Jacques de Vitry, *Historia occidentalis*
Salimbene   Salimbene di Adam, *Chronicles*

WRITINGS AND HAGIOGRAPHICAL SOURCES ON CLARE OF ASSISI

Proc   *Acts of the Process of Canonization of Clare of Assisi*
RsC   *Rule of Saint Clare* ("The Form of Life")
TestsC   *Testament of Saint Clare*

Contents

Translator's Note	9
Introduction	11
From Human Suffering to the Crucified Christ	15
A Great Family Drama	21
Can't You See My House Is Collapsing?	25
How What Was Bitter Became Sweet	29
Francis and the Confirmation of the Lord Pope	35
Excess Is Theft	43
Francis, Peace, and Arms	47
Strong in Weakness	51
When Francis Predicted the Earthquake	55
The Wound	59
The Poor King	63
That Blank Space without Notes	67
Listen, Poor Ladies	71
Saint Francis in Rieti	75
The Little Plant of Brother Francis	79
Beware of the Man, Not the Wolf	83
Francis and the Workers of the Eleventh Hour	87
The Magnet of Assisi	91
Blame the Tower of Babel	95
Saint Francis, the Most Italian of Saints	99
An Inclusive Vision: Saint Francis according to Pope Francis	103
The Choice to Be among the Marginalized	113
The Man Who Became Prayer	117
Conclusion	121
Notes	123

Translator's Note

Unless otherwise noted, all quotations from early documents by and about Francis of Assisi are taken from *Francis of Assisi: Early Documents (Vols. I–III)*, edited by Regis J. Armstrong, J. A. Wayne Hellmann, William J. Short, New York, New City Press, 1999–2002.

All quotations from early documents by and about Clare of Assisi are from *Clare of Assisi: Early Documents*, edited by Regis Armstrong, OFM Cap, New York, New City Press, 2006.

Quotations from the *Little Flowers of Saint Francis* are taken from *The Little Flowers of the Glorious Messer Saint Francis and of His Friars*, translated by W. Heywood, London, Howell Methuen & Co., 1906.

Quotations from Thomas of Eccleston's *De adventu F.F. minorum in Angliam* are taken from *The Friars and How They Came to England*, translated by Father Cuthbert, St. Louis, B. Herder, 1903.

Quotations from the *Divine Comedy* are taken from Dante Alighieri, *The Divine Comedy: Paradiso*, translated, with a commentary, by Charles S. Singleton; Bollingen Series LXXX, Princeton, Princeton University Press, 1975.

All biblical quotations are from the *Revised Standard Version Second Catholic Edition*.

Introduction

It is said in the book of the *Little Flowers of Saint Francis*:

> One day, as Saint Francis was returning from the forest, where he had been in prayer, the said Brother Masseo, wishing to test the humility of the saint, went forth to meet him exclaiming: "Why after thee? Why after thee?" To which Saint Francis made answer: "What is this? What meanest thou?" Brother Masseo answered: "I mean, why is it that all the world goeth after thee; why do all men wish to see thee, to hear thee, and to obey thy word? For thou art neither comely nor learned, nor art thou of noble birth. How is it, then, that all the world goeth after thee?"[1]

Brother Masseo could not understand how a man so physically unattractive could attract the attention of others more than bees to honey. And his question has not lost its relevance after so many centuries. Why do we all still follow Francis today? Why does his person know how to create consensus, even in a world like ours, long secularized and so alien to religious experience?

I think there is only one answer: The perennial relevance of Francis lies in the perennial newness of the Gospel. Jesus, the Word made flesh whom the Gospel communicates to us, is always beyond, always ahead of us, never outdated, always capable of subverting the mundane logic of "good sense." Whether we like it or not, Jesus continues to give hope to people of all times, or at least to stir them up, with his overwhelming life proposal. Francis, therefore, is relevant precisely because of his radical evangelism. In his experience, wrote Yves Marie-Joseph Congar (1904–1995), the absolute nature of the Christian Gospel is reflected.

It is true, though, that everything possible has been said about Francis, to the point of spreading an image of him that does not always correspond to reality. And it is also true that Francis's fame is often linked to facts and texts that have no historical consistency. If, for example, one asks an audience of nonspecialists what his most beautiful and significant writing is, many of them will answer that it is the so-called "Prayer of Saint Francis," a text that has nothing to do with the authentic Francis, and that came to light only in 1912, in a completely un-Franciscan context. Not to mention that one of the most famous episodes usually traced to the man from Assisi is still the delightful (but somewhat misrepresented) "little flower" of the Wolf of Gubbio. Many still believe that Francis and Clare were "a couple" before finding their vocations. And the examples could go on.

For more than thirty years now, the historical and spiritual personality of Francis of Assisi and the history of the religious family born from his experience have been the main object of my studies in the field of medieval history. This is a path along which I have always endeavored to seek — beyond the anecdotal and devotional — the man behind the saint.

Indeed, Francis's exceptionality, which his own contemporaries so strongly emphasized (to the point of transforming him into an *alter Christus*) has often ended up obscuring his humanity, making us forget that he was a flesh-and-blood person. For a long time a "little flower" image prevailed, one devoid of the vigor of everyday life. And yet it was precisely daily life, often so hard and contradictory, into which Francis immersed himself with all his heart, certain of the fact that the Son of God had become flesh and blood, sharing human experience with all its problems.

This approach is also present in the pages that follow, in which I collect the articles that I have published in *L'Osservatore Romano* over the years. I have often drawn inspiration from current events, as well as from the words and gestures of Pope Francis,[2] who, in taking the name of the Saint of Assisi, wanted to take a clear and irrevocable position. These are writings addressed to a wider audience, written in a more accessible style. Nevertheless, I have tried, as far as possible, to maintain methodological rigor, since making things accessible does not mean trivializing them. Instead it means making the results of research available to the greatest possible number of readers.

I have chosen to organize the articles, which have not undergone any substantial revision after their original publication, according to the timeline of Francis's life. At the end, I offer an analysis of the Franciscan vision of three people: Pope Francis; one of the most important voices of contemporary Italian poetry; and a historian who was doubtless among the greatest medievalists of the second half of the twentieth century.

It is good to keep in mind that historical research about Francis of Assisi constitutes a field of study that is both privileged and engaging — and therefore also dangerous. Privileged, because the research on the subject is by now very advanced, relying for a long time on a very solid group of expert researchers engaged in the field. It is engaging, because studying the historical Francis of Assisi and his spiritual experience is not the same as studying topics of pure economic history, if only because the Franciscan charism is still alive and vital. These same reasons, however, also make the field dangerous, since the advanced state of the research requires the scholar to commit to keeping constantly current. Moreover, when a research topic still maintains vital connections with the present and emotionally engages the scholar, there is always the risk of overlapping past and present and therefore distorting the past in view of the present.

Nevertheless, I am happy to have set out on this path, which over the years has given me so many scholarly joys and has made a great number and variety of encounters possible, in the worlds of both male and female consecrated life, in the cloistered and apostolic spheres, and in the even more diverse lay world.

In a famous passage (*Paradise* XI, 37), Dante wrote that Francis "was all seraphic in his ardor" (*FF* 2105). At that point and for the whole famous triplet, Alighieri, in reality, did not show a great originality: "The one [Francis] was all seraphic in ardor; / the other [Dominic] for wisdom on earth was / cherubic light a splendor." Indeed in his wonderful verse he did nothing but translate some words of Ubertino da Casale. In book V of his most famous work, *The Tree of the Crucified Life of Jesus*, in the third chapter, "Jesus Generates Francis," Ubertino had written: "Among these, the ones that shone brightest were Francis and Dominic, whose prototypes were Elijah and Henoch. The one was touched by the purifying coal of the Seraph and aflame with a heaven-sent ardor, so that he seemed to set the whole world alight. The other, like the Cherub with protecting wings outstretched, bright with the light of wisdom, prolific through his preaching, had a most radiant effect on a darkened world" (*FF* 2046).

Apart from these relationships of dependence, which I have recalled only out of a duty of justice — that is to say, in order to give each his due — there remains the affirmation that Francis burned with love of God, that he was "aflame with a heaven-sent ardor." Jacopone da Todi also spoke of a boundless love that flowed from the fiery heart of Francis, and admitted that he could not explain such an abundance of love: "I confess that I cannot explain such bounty / the boundless flow of the ardent heart" (*Lauda* 40, vv. 77–78: *FF* 2031). The words of Jesus come to mind, when the Master said that he "came to cast fire upon the earth" (Lk 12:49). If our personal answers were like the one Francis gave with his life, that fire would already be lit!

From Human Suffering to the Crucified Christ

Historians are in general agreement that in 1206, at the end of a long and complex process, Francis of Assisi's maturation in his conversion to Christ was complete. Thus began the extraordinary experience of holiness that has never ceased to exert its appeal throughout the centuries.

In his *Testament*, dictated shortly before his death, the saint himself judged his youthful conduct as sinful. He considered himself to have been a sinner before divine grace prompted him to review his values and criteria. Thomas of Celano, his first hagiographer, located the root of the young man's sins in the vanity that dominated him: Francis was vainglorious, desiring success in all things. Educated by his parents according to the vanity of the age, he grew even more vain and insolent than they, trying to excel over all his peers; his own prodigality was born of a great vanity (*1Cel* 1–2: *FF* 317, 320).

Even if the author of the *Legend of the Three Companions* has a completely different slant, he nevertheless substantially confirms Thomas's judgment. The unknown author of this work describes Francis's youthful habits with unusual realism. He tells us that Francis dressed in a showy and eccentric way, having clothes made for himself that were more sumptuous than his social status supposed. Ever in search of a new way to stand out, he went so far as to sew both precious fabrics and coarse cloths into the same garment (*3Comp* 2: *FF* 1396). As we can see, there is not much originality in the many fashion trends of recent years, which have had such a great impact on the rich and often bored young people of our Western world.

In another interesting aspect of the portrait of this rich young man, the *Legend* tells us that he reserved all his attention for his friends. When he had made plans with them, he would suddenly get up from the table, without even having finished eating, and leave his parents saddened by his sudden departure (*3Comp* 9: *FF* 1404). He was, therefore, a young man, focused on himself and his image, preoccupied with his friends, and inattentive to parents who nonetheless allowed him to be who he was and to spend even more than his condition would have permitted. A young man who was generous and jovial, but also eager to shock and make people talk about him, ultimately inattentive to the real problems of others. His very generosity toward the poor did not come from attention to their condition, but from adherence to the aristocratic code of conduct he had chosen: A young man who aspired to join the nobility could not be rude and ill-mannered toward the poor (*3Comp* 2: *FF* 1397).

This young man, far from God, nevertheless encountered human suffering. "When I was in sin," he said in the *Testament*, "it seemed too bitter for me to see lepers. And the Lord himself led me among them and *I showed mercy to them*. And when I left them, what had seemed bitter to me was turned into sweetness of soul and body. And afterwards I delayed a little and left the world" (*Test* 1–3: *FF* 110). In the *Legend of the Three Companions*, we are told that conversion began with a very hard struggle Francis had to fight with himself and with his city. The source marks out a series of six visits through which the Lord progressively revealed his plan to Francis and prepared him for the definitive revelation: life according to the form of the Gospel. Yet it was not an easy path.

After the first visits diverted him from his original dreams of glory and set him in search of God's will, while in prayer one day, he heard the voice of the Lord — we are at the fourth divine visit, according to the account of this precious hagiographic source — asking him to overturn his criteria and values, and leave behind all the things he had hitherto longed for. "Once you begin doing this," it was revealed to him, "what before seemed delightful and sweet will be unbearable and bitter; and what before made you shudder will offer you great sweetness and enormous delight" (*3Comp* 11: *FF 1407*).

A new phase had begun. Comforted by those words, Francis immediately committed himself to translating them into practice. While riding around Assisi, he happened upon a leper. He had always been horrified by lepers, but in that circumstance, doing violence to himself, he came down from his horse, kissed the hand of that man — perhaps covered with sores — and offered him money. Not only that, but he accepted the kiss of peace that the leper offered him in return (*3Comp* 11: *FF 1408*).

It was clearly a decisive moment. From then on, the *Legend* points out, he began to forget himself, until, with the grace of God, he came to govern himself perfectly. The Latin text (*magis ac magis*) gives a good idea of a pressure repeatedly exerted on himself. The young man tried to make attitudes and actions, which until some time before were repugnant to him, feel natural. That first victory strengthened him in his conviction and gave him new courage. A few days later, he took a considerable amount of money and went to the lepers' hospice where he gave them alms, kissing the hands of every sick person. His new victory brought him an unexpected gift: "What before had been bitter, that is, to see and touch lepers, was turned into sweetness" (ibid.). In the years of his carefree youth, Francis had been moved to pity at the fate of those poor unfortunates and had repeatedly given them alms. But he had limited himself to sending them through others. Now instead he didn't send alms but brought them in person, giving of himself. And only then did he receive in exchange that secret sweetness that no one and nothing in the world had ever been able to give him.

While he was immersed in this inner labor, the Lord again visited him, revealing to him that he would soon make him clearly understand what to do. He continued to go around with his friends, but by now he felt increasingly far from them, so much so that, to defend himself from their curiosity and that of others who pressed him with specific questions, he answered everyone in cryptic terms (*3Comp* 13: *FF* 1410).

A few days passed and the Lord visited him for the sixth time. Passing by the church of San Damiano, Francis felt compelled to enter. As he prayed fervently before the image of the Crucified One, he heard the voice of the Lord inviting him to repair his house. The young man interpreted those words in a material sense, aided by the very poor condition of that small country church. He therefore gave the priest money to buy oil to light a lamp in front of the crucifix. That intense interior experience, however, filled him with joy, radiantly illuminating him, since he felt within that it was Christ himself who had spoken to him (*3Comp* 13: *FF* 1411). Raoul Manselli has written that the encounter with the Crucified One in the church of San Damiano "places the suffering of Christ before the eyes of Francis and shows it to him as a superhuman value in the reality of human existence, as the sole force capable of giving meaning to and making sense of people's suffering, compelling them to seek it and to accept it with an act of free choice, in order to approach him."[1]

The event definitively sanctioned his exit from the world. He began to live with the poor, and like the poor, was misunderstood by his fellow citizens, who judged him to be out of his mind. All this brought with it a new, difficult struggle with himself. Raised among material comforts, delicate by nature, it was not easy for Francis to acquire the "qualities" necessary to live as a true poor man. In this regard, the *Legend of the Three Companions* reveals a precious detail: It specifies that the first followers approached Francis two years after his conversion (*3Comp* 27: *FF* 1429). He therefore remained in his city for two years, living among the derelict and, like them, begging for food in the streets he had traveled on horseback covered in precious fabrics, showing himself weak and submissive to those same people who had envied him for his wealth and who considered him destined for greatness. All this was not because of new social convictions, but as a consequence of the *sequela Christi*.

He chose, in fact, to follow Christ through the narrow door, trying to replicate, in his own existence, the choices and behaviors that were

Christ's during his own earthly sojourn. He chose and traveled to the end of the road he had taken, because now it was not his own self to guide him, but his desire to remain faithful to the will of God.

A Great Family Drama

The Synod on the Family proved to be important in many ways, not just pastorally. It also led us to reflect on the history of the domestic Church and its impact on people's lives. If Timothy, Paul's collaborator, received the first rudiments of faith and doctrine at home, transmitted to him by his mother Eunice and his grandmother Lois (2 Tim 1:5), other saints did not live in exemplary families. Francis of Assisi, as we know, was strongly opposed by his own family. One of the richest sources of information in this regard is undoubtedly the *Legend of the Three Companions.*

When the young man began to look at reality with new eyes, it says, "he proposed *in his heart,* from then on, never to deny alms to any poor person begging from him for God's sake, but rather to give more willingly and abundantly than usual" (*3Comp* 8: *FF* 1380).

From that moment on, some "oddities" of his also took shape, which Francis kept to himself, at least initially. On the other hand, after the inner conversation with the Crucified One in the church of San Damiano, he began to make his intense interior change public with sensational gestures. He loaded onto his horse a pack of fabric stolen from the store, and went to Foligno, where he sold it together with the horse. Seeing that his son had disappeared, his father began to search for him. When he heard this, Francis took refuge in a cave, where he stayed for a whole month. Only one member of the family knew that refuge and sometimes brought him food. The time spent in that cave was a further purification for Francis.

One day he left his refuge, drunk with enthusiasm. What followed is the wonderful picture of a great family drama. Immediately word of the chatter that accompanied him ran like sparks on a field of stubble, until it reached the ear of his father. As soon as he realized that the object of the public mockery was the very son who had for some time gave him nothing but problems, he fell upon him and dragged him home, where he locked him in a dark room, trying to bend Francis's will, first with words, then with beatings and chains (*3Comp* 17: *FF* 1417).

The family drama was taken to the streets, like the bad reality shows we are used to seeing today, in which the truth of those disputes that make the participants attack each other like beasts in the arena is doubtful. Here the drama was real, and knowing that it was on everyone's lips, after years of hard work — we don't know if it had always been honest, but it had certainly been hard — was no pleasure for Pietro, who had placed so much hope in that son. This only increased his pain and anger, which he could not help pouring out on Francis, the sole source of all his troubles.

Other family tensions emerged, however. While his father was away, Francis's mother realized that her son would not bend. She freed him from his captivity, which allowed him to return to San Damiano. When Pietro di Bernardone came back and realized the situation, he unleashed his anger on his wife, whose complicity had clearly come to light (*3Comp* 18: *FF* 1418). Tensions grew to the point where Francis's father arranged a trial against his son, who eventually stripped himself of everything before the bishop and his fellow citizens. The description of the state of mind of Pietro, who ended up cursing his son every time he met him, is very beautiful. But his was an anger that arose from intense pain, the consequence of a love that he believed was betrayed by that beloved son:

> When his father saw him in such disgrace, he was filled with unusual pain. Because he loved him dearly, he was ashamed and felt great sorrow for him. Seeing his flesh half-dead from excessive affliction and cold, he would curse him whenever he came upon him. (*3Comp* 23: *FF* 1423)

This lively and penetrating description conveys to the reader the awareness of a role reversal. The one in difficulty was not the young man, who had to deal with a harsh and bitter lifestyle to which he was not accustomed, but his father, who lived among creature comforts. Thus, while exalting the greatness of God, who gives strength to the weak, allowing them to conquer the strong, the author also instills human pity for a father who had loved his son poorly, but who nevertheless loved him and could not accept his own defeat.

Yet it was not only Pietro who suffered. Francis also felt acute pain when he found himself deprived of his father. The source points out that in considering the curses that his father flung at him, Francis turned to a poor and despised man and asked him to stay with him. He promised the man some of his alms if, at every curse, he would make the sign of the cross over Francis, giving him a blessing in place of a curse. It also specifies that Francis took that man as his father (*assumpsit sibi in patrem*), thus showing the young man's intimate need for a father figure. Even the words that Francis — according to the author — addressed to his father while the poor man was blessing him express this intimate need: "Don't you believe that God can give me a father to bless me against your curses?" (ibid.). How many times over the years did Francis return to the words of Psalm 27:10: "For my father and my mother have forsaken me, / but the Lord will take me up"? And what feelings must he have had?

Different and less traumatic, but no less harsh, was the clash with his brother. The *Legend* reports one, but it was likely not the only one. The author says that on a winter's day, while Francis was praying covered in poor rags, he passed by his brother, who — addressing another fellow citizen — uttered words of mockery about the new condition of his sibling. The latter, in turn, answered him in fervor of spirit, using the French language (ibid.).

Of course, life teaches that parents and children experience a rift in a family differently. A father remains a father and rarely forgets a son who has broken away from him, whatever the reason for that break. A brother, on the other hand, more easily distances himself from his brother when reasons for quarreling arise, to the point of forgetting about the other once a separation has taken place. The fact, therefore, that the author of the *Legend* does not depict strong emotions in this regard testifies not only to his ability to convey the psychology of his protagonists, but — primarily, I would say — to his narrative skill.

Francis, therefore, did not come from a perfect family, but from a family like any other, with its problems. With God's help, he faced a real path of reconciliation with himself and with others, which transformed him into someone completely at peace. His story testifies that, with God's help, anyone can do the same.

Can't You See My House Is Collapsing?

Strange as it may seem, the knowledge of the true form of the San Damiano Cross, the most reproduced depiction of the crucifix in the world, is a recent discovery. A documented study by Servus Gieben,[1] a Capuchin scholar who died in 2014, has made it clear that until the end of the nineteenth century that crucifix, of which many spoke and wrote, was in fact unknown to most people, at least in its appearance.

The oldest testimony on this subject says that Francis, still at the beginning of his journey of conversion, while spending a day

> walking by the church of San Damiano, he was told in the Spirit to go inside for a prayer. Once he entered, he began to pray intensely before an image of the Crucified, which spoke to him in a tender and kind voice: "Francis, don't you see that my house is being destroyed? Go, then, and rebuild it for me." Stunned and trembling, he said: "I will do so gladly, Lord." For he understood

that it was speaking about that church, which was near collapse because of its age. He was filled with such joy and became so radiant with light over that message, that he knew in his soul that it was truly Christ crucified who spoke to him.[2]

The church of San Damiano would later be inhabited by Clare and her sisters. Between 1257 and 1260, however, the nuns moved to the place where the mortal remains of their Mother rested, near the basilica being built in honor of the new saint (Clare had been canonized in 1255 by Alexander IV). In abandoning San Damiano, they brought with them that crucifix, before which they had prayed for so many years. Its accessibility thus became difficult, or perhaps those who dared to reproduce the San Damiano Cross did so without having direct knowledge of it. The fact remains that its depictions did not conform at all to the original, at least until a drawing by Juste de St. Fleury was made in 1882 and published in 1853.[3] In recent years, however, a silent and prayerful pause in front of the crucifix has become an essential and necessary stop on most pilgrimages to Assisi.

Still, that long parenthesis during which it was hidden from the eyes of the public generated doubt in some people about whether what is currently known and venerated is even the same crucifix of which the sources speak. This doubt resonated in the public, especially some years ago, in conjunction with the anniversary of the conversion of Francis of Assisi (2006), when that crucifix returned to the center of attention.

There are testimonies, however, that allow us to dispel any possible doubts in this regard. Two of them are taken from the volume of *Fonti Clariane*, the true *summa* of medieval testimonies about Saint Clare of Assisi, published in 2013 by Giovanni Boccali. The first notice can be found in *ms. Assisano 344*, a codex of the second half of the fourteenth century, written in part by Fra Giovanni Ioli, librarian of the *Sacro Convento* of Assisi. The first part contains the *Tractatus* of Fra Francesco Bartoli on the indulgence of the Portiuncula. It then records some information on indulgences and relics related to the church of San Damiano. Among other things, it notes (f. 63r) that some reliquaries, previously kept in San Damiano, were at the time "preserved honorably with the sacred relics in Santa Chiara d'Assisi, along with the crucifix that spoke to Blessed Francis in the church of San Damiano" (*Fonti clariane*, no. 2124).

The second, and to me even more important one, is found in an illuminated codex of the second half of the fifteenth century containing the *Legenda Major* of Bonaventure in Middle High German. The text and miniatures are attributed to the Poor Clare Sibylla de Bondorff, who, in the second half of the fifteenth century and at the beginning of the next century, was active as a miniaturist and copyist in the monasteries of Freiburg and Strasbourg. In this same codex, an anonymous Poor Clare added some news after her death. Among these, the detailed testimony of Conrad de Bondorff, who assured us that the crucifix that spoke to Saint Francis was still

> kept with great reverence in the monastery where our most blessed mother Saint Clare physically rests. It is painted on wood, and is not a carved image; it is flat and not raised. And when Christ spoke to him from the image, saying three times, "Francis, go, repair my house which is now collapsing," then the head was lifted from the painting, just as the carved crucifixes are normally lifted. So even today, in these days, the face is lifted from the painting. ... And this was seen by the venerable, highly learned doctor and reverend father, guardian of Lake Constance, then reader in Strasbourg, Friar Conrad de Bondorff, who said that it was an ugly painting, old and faded, but the face was fair and venerable. And this had been seen on the eve of our mother Saint Clare [August 10], when the year after the birth of Christ 1473 was counted.[4]

The oldest testimony about the nuns' jealous custody of the Crucified One, however, is contained in a sermon by Saint Bonaventure, delivered a few years after Clare's death. This is Sermon 57, which until now was known only in the editions edited by the Quaracchi fathers (1901) and Father Jacques Guy Bougerol (Paris 1993), based on the Troyes codex, *Médiatheque*, ms. 951. Only recently, however, has Aleksander Horowski[5] made known a passage from the same sermon in the version transmitted by the Berlin codex, *Staatsbibliothek, Theol. Lat. Octavo* 31, extremely interesting for our purposes. In fact, in the Troyes version, Christ is said to have spoken to Francis from the cross not as a stranger, but as a close friend, according to what was reported by the sisters of San Damiano (*ut servatur a sororibus Sancti Damiani*). Whereas the Berlin version (f. 47rb) — transcribed, of course, by a different listener — says that Christ spoke to him not in an ordinary way, i.e., through inner locution (*per internam inspirationem*), but in a very particular way, since that crucifix which was kept by the nuns of San Damiano (*quem adhuc tenent moniales Sancti Damiani*) asked him to repair the church with a perceptible voice.

Authoritative testimonies therefore document that the Poor Clares always preserved the crucifix that spoke to Saint Francis, which is the very one currently on display in the Basilica of Santa Chiara in Assisi, in the chapel of San Giorgio. Even today that image speaks to the hearts of many, as one day it spoke to the heart of the saint.

How What Was Bitter Became Sweet

The theme of mercy has characterized the pontificate of Pope Francis from the beginning. In his first Angelus, on Sunday, March 17, 2013, commenting on the episode of the adulterous woman saved by Jesus (Jn 8:1–11), he recalled that "God's face is the face of a merciful father who is always patient." Then, reporting words that had been addressed to him by a woman in her eighties, he reiterated that the Lord "never tires of forgiving, but at times we get tired of asking for forgiveness." A few weeks later, to the priests he ordained on the fourth Sunday of Easter, the Sunday of the Good Shepherd (April 21, 2013), he asked, "In the name of Christ and the Church, never tire of being merciful." And many other examples could be easily found. If the decision to call an extraordinary jubilee, the Holy Year of Mercy, is an unexpected and joyful event, it is nevertheless in keeping with the actions of this pope, who is as extraordinary as his jubilee.

In order to better understand the meaning of this proposal, I believe it is useful to ask ourselves in what terms Francis of Assisi — the saint from whom the pope took his name — spoke of mercy and how he lived it. In dictating his *Testament* shortly before his death, Francis defined his encounter with the lepers as the major moment of his conversion and condemned the way he had dealt with them in his youth. "The Lord gave me, Brother Francis, thus to begin doing penance in this way: for when I was in sin, it seemed too bitter for me to see lepers. And the Lord himself led me among them and *I showed mercy to them*. And when I left them, what had seemed bitter to me was turned into sweetness of soul and body. And afterwards I delayed a little and left the world" (*Test* 1-3: *FF* 110). He thus characterized the beginning of his conversion as "doing mercy." From self-centeredness — this was, in essence, the root of his youthful sins — he became capable of looking at the problems of others so as to share, even externally, the lives of those who to him represented the living presence of Christ in history. "Think of the human suffering," wrote Raoul Manselli, "the unparalleled humiliation of the son of the rich merchant, who accepts to descend to the rank of those who had been the object of his pity and mercy."[1]

Out of that experience of mercy, a new man was born, one capable of overturning criteria of value and judgment. Bitterness became sweetness and what was once abhorrent became the reason for life, until he himself became an instrument of mercy. In all probability, Francis wrote his *Letter to a Minister* in the months preceding the Chapter of 1223, during which the text of the Rule to be submitted for papal approval was revised. To the minister — obviously laid low by clashes with friars that his role of responsibility did not spare him — Francis pointed out that the path was not separation from his brothers, but a total immersion in brotherhood, devoid of any defense and of any expectation toward others. He then sank the scalpel further into the wound:

> And if you have done this, I wish to know in this way if you love the Lord and me, his servant and yours: that there is not any brother in the world who has sinned — however much he could have sinned — who, after he has looked into your eyes, would ever depart without your mercy, if he is looking for mercy. And if he were not looking for mercy, you would ask him if he wants

mercy. And if he would sin a thousand times before your eyes, love him more than me so that you may draw him to the Lord; and always be merciful with brothers such as these.[2]

In keeping with the gospel commandment (Mt 18:22), Francis therefore asked the minister to forgive sincerely, from the bottom of his heart. The sinning brother should not hear words of forgiveness, since it is easier to lie with words, but read his forgiveness in the offended minister's eyes, with which it is more difficult to lie. And not only that! If the sinful friar had not done so, the minister himself should ask his brother if he wanted to receive mercy, and should love him even more than Francis himself, with the sole aim of drawing him to the Lord, since the salvation of the brothers was the most precious good of all. On the other hand, was it not written in the first Rule that the brothers should "express the love they have for one another by their deeds" (*Rnb* XI, 6: *FF* 37)?

Francis then concluded, "And you may announce this to the guardians, when you can, that, for your part, you are resolved to act in this way" (*Lmin* 12: *FF* 236). The minister had then to commit himself publicly to this uphill path, thus putting himself in the hands of any detractors who, at any moment, could reproach him for not being perfectly consistent with his announced intention. He was asked for a ministry of mercy, with the ultimate goal of eliciting mercy.

In the second part of the letter, attaching a text that he believed should have been included in the Rule, a text which the Chapter then greatly amended, Francis again asked all the brothers who had learned of the sin of a brother to "show great mercy to him": "*those who are well do not need a physician, but the sick do.*" The custodian would also have to provide "mercifully" for the sinful friar, "as he would wish to be provided for were he in a similar position." All the friars were to show great mercy to the sinful friar and keep his sin secret (*Lmin* 15–16.18: *FF* 237).

Francis, however, insisted on mercy, almost giving the impression of wanting to go overboard. For, says Saint James, "judgment is without mercy to one who has shown no mercy; yet mercy triumphs over judgment" (Jas 2:13). And as proof of the fact that he had this biblical text in mind, he expressly mentions it in the second version of the so-called *Letter to the Faithful*, perhaps the last to be written in his epistolary. Addressing all Christians, Francis admonished:

> Let whoever has received the power of judging others pass judgment with mercy, as they would wish to receive mercy from the Lord. For *judgment will be without mercy* for those *who have not shown mercy*. (2Lf 28–29: FF 191)

And again:

> Instead, let the one to whom obedience has been entrusted and *who is* considered *the greater* be *the lesser* and the servant of the other brothers. And let him have and show mercy to each of his brothers as he would want them to do to him were he in a similar position. Let him not become angry at the fault of a brother but, with all patience and humility, let him admonish and support him. (2Lf 42–44: FF 197–198)

It was a peaceful man who wrote such things, one capable at times of transmitting an extraordinary interior peace, as shown by his next-to-last admonition, which echoes the speeches he made to his brothers in the last years of his life:

> Where there is charity and wisdom, / there is neither fear nor ignorance (*Adm* XXVI: FF 197–198). Where there is patience and humility, / there is neither anger nor disturbance. / Where there is poverty with joy, / there is neither covetousness nor greed. / Where there is rest and meditation, / there is neither anxiety nor restlessness. / Where there is fear of the Lord to guard an entrance, / there the enemy cannot have a place to enter. / *Where there is a heart full of mercy and discernment, / there is neither excess nor hardness of heart.* (*Adm* XXVII: FF 177, emphasis added)

As we said, the Francis who emerges from this is a peaceful man, forged by suffering, inflamed with love for Christ, eager to communicate the salvation obtained by the Lord to all. He is a man of Easter, who experienced the cross to the point of living in his flesh the piercing of nails, who wrestled with the Lord face to face, who also had his moments of weakness and suffered the trial of tremendous temptations, but who remained faithful, because he who had his body delivered to death for our sake was faithful.

For this reason he was able to rejoice in life, because he had fully understood its value. He knew that everything passes; that it is unwise therefore, to focus on things, for God alone remains.

Francis and the Confirmation of the Lord Pope

Francis, a new name! The decision to name his son that, after his wife had given him the much more popular name of Giovanni, is owed to Pietro di Bernardone, and it must be said immediately that, if not completely new, it was not among those commonly used. It was a "new" name, therefore, just as the life experience of the saint of Assisi was new. In the same way, Jorge Bergoglio's choice to assume the name of Francis, a name until now used more by sovereigns than by popes, is completely new in the history of the Church. And it shows on his part a precise and decisive choice, as he himself made clear during his meeting with journalists on Saturday, March 16, 2013.

He placed Francis, therefore, at the heart of the Roman Church, to which the man from Assisi always professed unconditional devotion.

Francis the saint combined, in fact, the choice of Christ and his following with a clear and decisive choice of obedience and orthodoxy. His declarations in this regard are too many and too clear to leave room for doubt. The sequence of events that he marked out in his *Testament* seems emblematic to me. One cannot help but notice that in the first part of the *Testament*, the so-called "biographical" part, Francis made explicit reference seven times to an intervention of God in his vocational history. He thus endeavored to make the friars understand that the fundamental steps of his existence had been guided by God, that it was his initiative to which Francis responded with docility.

Francis, nevertheless, submitted that religious intuition, revealed to him by the Lord, to the discernment of the Apostolic See. We have to carefully consider the value of his gesture, which would have profound repercussions for the history of the primitive *fraternitas* and the subsequent Franciscan order. What is striking in the account of the *Testament*, in fact, is the direct temporal connection the saint established between the revelation of life according to the form of the Gospel and the decision to submit to the pope's discernment the purpose of the life he and his men had progressively formed following that revelation. "And after the Lord gave me some brothers, no one showed me what I had to do, but the Most High himself revealed to me that I should live according to the pattern of the Holy Gospel. And I had this written down simply and in a few words and the Lord Pope confirmed it for me" (*Test* 14–15: *FF* 116).

In the memory of the Franciscan order, the meeting with Innocent III took on a value of absolute importance. It is opportune to ask oneself, however, what it was in reality. Thomas of Celano, who could not benefit from the testimony of Francis's companions, provided a version of the facts that presented no difficulty (*1Cel* 32–33: *FF* 372–376), at least on the papal side, and his account was also used by other authors who wrote shortly after 1230. Giovanni da Perugia, author of the work *Beginning or Foundation of the Order (Anonymous Perugian)*, who wrote before 1241, relying on eyewitnesses (Bernard and Giles, first of all), tried to correct Celano's version (*Anper* 31–36: *FF* 1523–1529). These two traditions were the inspiration for subsequent authors, who brought nothing new of substance, other than further prodigious signs, rewriting the facts within their overall perspective. All this makes it difficult to determine the course of events with absolute precision, although it is possible to establish the essential moments.

It was above all preaching that prompted Francis and his men to go to the pope. The hypothesis seems to be confirmed not only by the many references contained in the Franciscan sources, but also by what Roger of Wendover, a monk of the English abbey of Saint Alban, who died in 1236, states in one of his enjoyable stories. According to Roger, the pope said to Francis:

> Go, brother, and look for some pigs, to whom you are more fit to be compared rather than to human beings, and roll around with them in a slough; give them this Rule you prepared and fulfill there your office of preaching.

Ultimately though, Innocent III confirmed "the office of preaching" (*FF* 2285–2286).

Innocent III's first reaction was not positive. The account of the so-called *Anonimo perugino* seems to be more reliable than other sources in this regard, not only because it is more in line with the normal actions of the Roman Curia, but also because Thomas himself confirms that the consent of the pontiff resulted in a prudent willingness to wait for the development of events.

The initial attitude of rejection on the part of Innocent III is confirmed in an addition included in the *Legenda Major* thanks to Girolamo da Ascoli, successor of Bonaventure of Bagnoregio as the head of the order (1274–1279) and then Pope Nicholas IV (1288–1292). It specifies that the meeting between the two took place in the part of the Lateran Palace called *Speculum* and that the pontiff, absorbed in deep meditations, drove the servant of Christ (who was unknown to him) away with indignation (*LegM* III, 9a: *FF* 1063).

Innocent III's reception, on the one hand, must therefore be scaled down. But it is precisely his wait-and-see attitude — which confirms, to some extent, a flexibility already manifested in other circumstances — that changed the course of events. And this was one of the aspects, and certainly not a minor one, of the greatness of this pope.

From then on, the text that had been presented to the pontiff began to get progressively richer. In its drafting, the friars continued with the criterion they had followed to that point: The text would be drawn up with the help of all, because all shared in the experience of life in which they were engaged. The friars, who met annually in Assisi for the Chapter, reflected on the basic reasons for their choice, examined the problems with which they had come into contact as they traveled the world, and set down in writing some basic norms. In the years that followed, they submitted those same precepts to revision, integrating, retouching, and correcting what had been previously written down.

Raniero Capocci, Cardinal Deacon of Santa Maria in Cosmedin (*Jordan* 16: *FF* 2339), was present at the General Chapter held in Assisi on Pentecost 1221. On that occasion, with the consent of the friars gathered in the assembly, the text of the Rule as it had been articulated over time was completed. However, that drafting, which has gone down in history as the *Regula Non Bullata*, did not obtain papal approval. Nevertheless, in some way, 1221 also represented a new starting point, since work continued on the final approval. The *Letter to a Minister* is an eloquent testimony to this incessant work. Those were difficult years, with repeated clashes between Francis and the friars, especially with the ministers and those from university circles. Many conflicts arose precisely around the drafting of the text of the Rule. In any case, the definitive sanction of the proposal of Franciscan life was reached, codified in the text sealed by Honorius III on November 29, 1223, with the letter *Solet annuere*.

The text opens and closes with the arduous affirmation that the friars are bound to observe the Gospel: "The Rule and Life of the Lesser Brothers is this: to observe the Holy Gospel of Our Lord Jesus Christ" (*Rb* I, 1: *FF* 75); "so that ... we may observe the poverty and humility and the holy Gospel of our Lord Jesus Christ, which we have firmly promised" (*Rb* XII, 4: *FF* 109). The inclusion of all of this seems therefore to be central, and this commitment is the hermeneutical key to understanding its most authentic meaning. A modern reader might wonder whether this, far from being a conscious choice of the friars who authored the text, is instead the result of a speculation of modern scholars, whose eagerness for "original" readings comes from an urge for novelty.

It is true, however, that one of the "Leonine" texts betrayed by the so-called *Assisi Compilation* refers to some words of Francis, who, in contrast with the ministers, reportedly said:

> That all the brothers may know that they are bound to observe the perfection of the holy Gospel, I want it written at the beginning and at the end of the *Rule* that the brothers are bound to observe the holy Gospel of our Lord Jesus Christ. (*CAs* 102: *FF* 1645)

And we must also remember that it is not by chance that the second and penultimate affirmations of the Rule coincide in proclaiming the friars' full communion and obedience to the Roman Catholic Church, and in particular to the successor of Peter, visible and present in the order through the figure of the cardinal protector. "Brother Francis promises obedience and reverence to our Lord Pope Honorius and his successors canonically elected and to the Roman Church" (*Rb* I, 2: *FF* 76); "so that, being always submissive and subject at the feet of the same Holy Church and steadfast in the Catholic Faith, we may observe" (*Rb* XII, 4: *FF* 109). The life of the fraternity is thus concretized in the program of observing poverty and humility and the Gospel of Jesus Christ, in communion with and obedience to the Roman Church. The text, which is the fruit of different hands, undoubtedly reflects the souls who collaborated in its drafting. Nevertheless, the footsteps of the man from Assisi remain indelibly imprinted on it, certainly visible in some expressions and in the repetition of some first-person verbs characteristic of its lexicon. This is shown by the fact that they are identical in other writings which are undoubtedly his own.

The *Regula Bullata* codified, as far as possible for a written text, the richness of the Franciscan ideal. Honorius III's confirmation made the text now definitive, conclusive, and no longer perfectible. Nevertheless, due to one of those paradoxes that often characterize the lives of men, even ones as exceptional as Francis of Assisi, the very achievement of this goal, to which he had dedicated considerable energy, seems to mark the beginning of a new restlessness for him.

Rapid and continuous changes, as well as tensions that had not been properly resolved, finally led him to intervene and to dictate the *Testa-

ment which, according to his own words, was specifically aimed at urging the brothers to observe the Rule promised to the Lord "more catholicly" (*Test* 34: *FF* 127).

In the first half of the 1220s, the Friars Minor had become more and more involved in pastoral activity. At the same time, the priestly element had grown in number and acquired progressive importance within the order. Being part of pastoral activity meant preaching, celebrating Mass, and hearing confessions of the people.

The Church needed evangelizers. Many asked that the friars also collaborate in this worthy work. Substantial sectors within the order and some men of the Roman Curia who were more sensitive to the work of reform pressed in this direction. Nevertheless, by taking part in pastoral activity, the Minors inevitably ended up in conflict with the episcopate (*Rb* IX, 1: *FF* 98). An itinerant order, moreover, could easily avoid outside control, and this naturally led to the rise of prejudices and concerns.

How can we, therefore, fail to give credit, at least in substance, to the situation described in a famous passage from the Leonine tradition, and reported by the *Assisi Compilation* and by many other sources? In it, Leo, the faithful companion of the saint, testifies that some friars said to Francis: "Father, don't you see that sometimes bishops do not permit us to preach, allowing us to remain idle in an area for many days before we can preach to the people? It would be better if you arranged for the brothers to get a privilege from the Lord Pope: it would be the salvation of souls." He answered this proposal with a clear refusal, concluding, "I want only this privilege from the Lord: not to have any privilege from any human being, except to show reverence to all, and, by the obedience of the holy *Rule*, to convert everyone more by example than by word" (*CAs* 20: *FF* 1565).

With the *Testament* Francis therefore indicated a different way. In this context, his statements are full of significance:

> The Lord gave me, and gives me still, such faith in priests who live according to the rite of the holy Roman Church because of their orders that, were they to persecute me, I would still want to have recourse to them. And if I had as much *wisdom* as *Solo-*

mon and found impoverished priests of this world, I would not preach in their parishes against their will. (*Test* 6–7: *FF* 112)

There are other significant expressions, taken from a wider section (*Test* 4–13: *FF* 111–115) that pivots on the person of the priest, in which Francis strongly reaffirms his full fidelity and submission to the Church of Rome. Priests are to be welcomed and venerated regardless of their frailty and contradictions, which are completely human. They are to be looked upon with eyes of faith, "because, of the Most High Son of God himself" we see nothing "bodily in this world other than the most holy Body and his most holy Blood, which they receive and which they alone administer to others" (*Test* 10: *FF* 113).

Francis's existence was therefore guided by faith: not just any type of faith in any type of God, but faith in the God of Jesus Christ transmitted and preserved by the Roman Church. He wanted to entrust himself and his religious family to the Church of Rome, requiring the brothers to ask "our Lord the Pope for one of the Cardinals of the Holy Roman Church," as "governor, protector and corrector," so that "being always submissive and subject at the feet of the same Holy Church and steadfast in the Catholic Faith," they might observe "the poverty and humility and the holy Gospel of the Lord Jesus Christ," which they "firmly promised" (*Rb* XII, 3–4: *FF* 108–109). In this faith he lived and died.

Excess Is Theft

Some gestures of charity by Pope Francis, made through the apostolic almoner, Cardinal Konrad Krajewski, have triggered a broader reflection on the meaning of almsgiving and its practice in the life of the Church.

The question, in reality, has always been alive, because it is an essential aspect of the wider problem of Christians' relationship with temporal wealth and goods, themes on which Jesus focused. The Fathers of the Church expressed the conviction that God had destined the goods of the earth to all men, not just to some. For this reason, many of them believed that the surplus of the few had somehow been taken away from the needs of the many. Basil the Great, in his famous homily on avarice, clearly stated, "The goods you have received to distribute to all, you have hoarded. Whoever strips a man of his clothes is called a marauder, and whoever does not dress the naked man, being able to do so, what other name does he deserve? To the hungry belongs the bread you hide; to the naked is the cloak that you keep in your closets; to the barefoot the sandals that grow moldy around you; to the poor is the money that you lock up."[1] He was echoed in the West by Gregory the Great, who exerted so much influence during the Middle Ages. In fact, the Holy Pontiff affirmed in his *Pastoral Rule* (III, 21) that in giving the poor what they need, we do not give them what is ours, but we give them back what is theirs.

This teaching was very present at the Second Vatican Council. The council fathers, in a passage from *Gaudium et Spes*, expressed the conviction that

> under the leadership of justice and in the company of charity, created goods should be in abundance for all in like manner. ... Man should regard the external things that he legitimately possesses not only as his own but also as common in the sense that they should be able to benefit not only him but also others. ... The Fathers and Doctors of the Church held this opinion, teaching that men are obliged to come to the relief of the poor and to do so not merely out of their superfluous goods. If one is in extreme necessity, he has the right to procure for himself what he needs out of the riches of others. Since there are so many people prostrate with hunger in the world, this sacred council urges all, both individuals and governments, to remember the aphorism of the Fathers, "Feed the man dying of hunger, because if you have not fed him, you have killed him," and really to share and employ their earthly goods, according to the ability of each, especially by supporting individuals or peoples with the aid by which they may be able to help and develop themselves.[2]

Almsgiving, in this way, is qualified as restitution: restitution to the poor of what has been unduly taken away from them.

The legacy of the great patristic tradition is also evident in the gestures and teaching of Francis of Assisi. In the *Regula Non Bullata*, he asked those brothers who were forced by necessity to go begging, not to be ashamed, but to remember

> that our Lord Jesus Christ, the Son of the all-powerful living God, set his face like flint and was not ashamed. He was poor

and a stranger and lived on alms — he, the Blessed Virgin, and his disciples. When people revile them and refuse to give them alms, let them thank God for this because they will receive great honor before the tribunal of our Lord Jesus Christ for such insults. Let them realize that a reproach is imputed not to those who suffer it but to those who caused it. *Alms are a legacy and a justice due to the poor* that our Lord Jesus Christ acquired for us.[3]

Almsgiving, therefore, is justice due to the poor. For the man from Assisi, too, surplus came to be qualified as theft. The idea returns in a saying attributed to him by Brother Leo, who assures us that Francis "often said these words to the brothers: 'I have never been a thief, that is, in regard to alms, which are the inheritance of the poor. I always took less than I needed, so that other poor people would not be cheated of their share. To act otherwise would be theft (*contrarium facere furtum esset*)'" (*CAs* 15: *FF* 1561).

It is true, of course, that many of the so-called Leonine passages are characterized by a strong polemical content. In fact, the saying of Francis on almsgiving appeared as a clear reminder against the danger arising from seeking donations, which for some time had become the ordinary means of subsistence of the friars. In this way it was possible for them to even amass considerable reserves, without fearing daily precariousness. It reveals, however, an extraordinary consonance, not only in terms of content, but also in terminology, with what is affirmed in the *Regula Non Bullata*.

Similar concepts, also expressed with similar words, have been attributed to Clare of Assisi, as the testimony given by Cristiana di Bernardo da Suppo in her process of canonization reveals. She reported that when the saint, eager to follow in the footsteps of Christ, was preparing to sell off her inheritance, her relatives "wanted her to give them a better price. She did not want to sell it to them, but sold it to others so the poor would not be defrauded. All she received from the sale of the inheritance, she distributed to the poor. Asked how she knew this, she replied: because she saw and heard it" (*Proc* XIII, 11: *FF* 3104).

Is it therefore so outrageous to think that in the aforementioned account Brother Leo could have referred to words actually spoken — at least in their substance — by Francis himself? This conviction, indeed, appears to be confirmed by a series of episodes reported by sources which it seems difficult to doubt.

There are strong statements, therefore, both from the Fathers and from the saints of the Middle Ages, as well as from the recent Magisterium of the Church. Some will perhaps consider them exaggerated, in the conviction that the saints often lack common sense. In reality, it is we ordinary people, albeit practicing believers, who use the excuse of good sense to often trample on the Gospel.

Francis, Peace, and Arms

In a brilliant and richly documented essay, Sandra Migliore illustrated, years ago, the various rereadings which the figure of Francis of Assisi underwent between the nineteenth and twentieth centuries, often with different and even opposite results, readings frequently motivated by partisan interests.[1] In fact, Francis never ceases to make people talk about him, and in every age his biography has been able to amaze and disturb people.

So, even faced with an era like ours, shaken by so many conflicts, some in the spotlight daily, many others — alas! — sadly and shamefully forgotten, his teachings can offer us some useful food for thought. What was, in fact, his thinking, his way of confronting war and peace, the death of the defenseless and the power of arms?

In reality, Francis too had been a man of arms in his youth. He saw combat against the Perugians in the battle of Collestrada, during which he was taken prisoner. The harsh experience of imprisonment, however, did not discourage him. He even dreamed of undertaking new military adventures, in the hope of obtaining glory and higher social status. He, a bourgeois, wanted to rise to the rank of knight — that is to say, to gain a noble title. Then he met the Lord, like Paul on the road to Damascus. It was not — as it was for the Apostle — a bolt out of the blue, but a progressive inner distillation, which led him, finally, from a self-centered existence to total forgetfulness of self. He understood then that he should not seek his own glory, but the glory of God, of that "Prince of Peace" (Is 9:6) who had come to bring the peace that the world cannot give (Jn 14:27) and who asked him to sheath his sword (Mt 26:52). He became aware of the fact that only the Lord could give men peace, once they were willing to defuse the explosive mechanisms nested in their inner universe. This conviction is fully evident in his writings.

In the *Regula Non Bullata*, completed in 1221, it states, "When the brothers go through the world, let them take *nothing*. ... Let them not resist anyone evil, but whoever strikes them on one cheek, let them offer him the other as well" (*Rnb* XIV, 1–4: *FF* 40). In the *Regula Bullata* (1223) they are still asked "to have humility and patience in persecution and infirmity, and to love those who persecute, rebuke, and find fault with us" (*Rb* X, 9–10: *FF* 104). And in the famous *Canticle of the Sun*, Brother Francis exclaims: "Praised be you, my Lord, through those who give pardon for your love, and bear infirmity and tribulation" (*Cant* 10: *FF* 263).

Shortly before Pentecost, 1223, writing to a friar in charge of other friars who made him suffer greatly, Francis proposed the paradoxical and disarming logic of the Gospel:

> I speak to you, as best I can, about the state of your soul. You must consider as grace all that impedes you from loving the Lord God and whoever has become an impediment to you, whether brothers or others, even if they lay hands on you. And may you want it to be this way and not otherwise. And let this be for you the true obedience of the Lord God and my true obedience, for I know with certitude that it is true obedience. And love those who do those things to you and do not wish anything different from them, unless it is something the Lord God shall have given you. And love them in this and do not wish that they be better Christians.[2]

Chapter XVI of the *Regula Non Bullata* is interesting in this regard. It was most likely written after the experience of Francis in the Holy Land, therefore between 1220 and 1221. Those friars who, by divine inspiration, wanted to go among the infidels could "live spiritually among the Saracens and nonbelievers in two ways. One way is not to engage in arguments or disputes but to be subject to every human creature for God's sake and to acknowledge that they are Christians. The other way is to announce the Word of God, when they see it pleases the Lord, in order that [unbelievers] may believe in almighty God, the Father, the Son and the Holy Spirit" (*Rnb* XVI, 5–7: *FF* 43). Therefore, only after they had ensured that it was pleasing to the Lord could the friars evangelize, announcing to the Muslims the Trinitarian Faith. Whereas it was always possible to lead a hidden life, without exposing themselves in any other way except through an unvoiced and silent witness, promoting neither quarrels nor debates, and subservient to every creature. Not only that, but in that same chapter, all the brothers are reminded that "wherever they are" they have given themselves and abandoned their bodies to our Lord Jesus Christ. And for his love they must expose themselves to enemies, both visible and invisible, for the Lord says: "*Whoever loses his life because of me will save it in eternal life*" (*Rnb* XVI, 10–11: *FF* 45).

All the testimonies agree that, during his sojourn overseas, the saint used only the Word of God, "sharper than any two-edged sword" (Heb 4:12); a Word preached to Saladin's nephew, Malik al-Kamil, who did not convert to Christianity, as Francis hoped, but was able to listen, showing himself to be magnanimous and tolerant. This encounter caused amazement, to the point that not only Christian sources, but also Islamic ones, bear some — albeit weak — trace of it.

Unlike the rules of the military orders, the Franciscan Rule never mentions arms, for a very simple reason: Weapons were foreign to the mental universe of Francis and his companions. After his conversion, for the rest of his life, the man from Assisi was an apostle of peace:

> In all of his preaching before he presented the word of God to the assembly, he prayed for peace saying, "May the Lord give you peace." He always proclaimed this to men and women, to those

he met and to those who met him. Accordingly, many who hated peace along with salvation, with the Lord's help wholeheartedly embraced peace. They became themselves children of peace, now rivals for eternal salvation. (*1Cel* 23: *FF* 359)

Other ancient testimonies confirm these statements of his first hagiographer.[3]

His teaching is clear, both in theory and in practice. It is enough to think that it would be just a few years after the death of Francis, in 1233, that Franciscans and Dominicans actively engaged in a great peace campaign (known as the "*Alleluia* Movement") involving several cities in northern and central Italy. In many cases, it resulted in the adoption of new city statutes, an event that showed how a social leaven could spark the evangelical utopia.

It is true, however, that conditions change over time, that people change and history seeks new answers. In the eight centuries of their history, alongside Franciscans committed to making their active and effective contribution to the establishment of peace, we find others who did not hesitate to personally engage in episodes of warfare. So it was that, perhaps a few years after 1233 (it is impossible to establish a precise date), Brother Leone da Perego, who had been very active at the time of the *Alleluia* and had been archbishop of Milan since 1241, personally bore the banner at the head of the Milanese army that went to battle against the troops of Emperor Frederick II.[4] And it is also true that in the second half of the thirteenth century, another friar, Fidenzio da Padova, drew up an actual plan, complete with military strategies, to reconquer the Holy Land.[5] The examples, of course, could be multiplied, in one direction and in the other.

It is undoubtedly a story that is complex and difficult to write. It is a story not of heroes and villains, but of people equally convinced of interpreting the will of God who, in different situations from time to time, gave different responses to similar problems.

Strong in Weakness

The journey of Pope Francis to the Holy Land, fifty years after the historic pilgrimage of Paul VI, brought to mind the journey of another Francis, the Saint of Assisi, who left for overseas lands in 1219. Francis loved Christ above all and above everyone, aware that the gift of faith, rediscovered in adulthood after a lacerating — and liberating — encounter with human suffering, was the most important gift he received in life. Some current reinterpretations aim to present his religious experience through an irenic filter, as if in Francis's eyes one experience of faith was the same as the other, as long as the believer sincerely loved his Lord. They thus seem reductive and do not correspond to the truth. Nevertheless, his experience of faith was undoubtedly original: In difficult times, he took a different path, pointing out to the brothers who "by divine inspiration" had asked to go "among the Saracens and nonbelievers" (*Rnb* XVI, 3: *FF* 42), an ideal of silent and peaceful witness, which did not even have proselytism as a core feature.

In 1219, therefore, he set out, bringing with him a brother, Illuminato (*LegM* IX, 8: *FF* 1173). The experience of the man from Assisi did not pass unnoticed. It left traces not only in the *Lives* dedicated to him in the course of the thirteenth century — which was to be expected — but also in non-Franciscan authors and even in sources of Islamic origin, as the great French Islamist Louis Massignon was able to prove several decades ago. The oldest Christian testimony is a letter from Jacques de Vitry, a Brabant prelate whom Innocent III had appointed Bishop of Acre (Tolemaide) in 1216.

In 1220, in a letter addressed to Pope Honorius III (among others), the prelate expressed sadness because some of his clerics had abandoned him to join the Friars Minor. Nevertheless, in speaking of their founder, he could not avoid showing a point of admiration. "The head of these brothers," he wrote, "who also founded the order, came into our camp. He was so inflamed with zeal for the Faith that he did not fear to cross the lines to the army of our enemy. For several days he preached the Word of God to the Saracens and made a little progress" (*2Vitry* 2: *FF* 2212).

It cannot be said that the expedition was carefully planned. Certainly, Giordano da Giano's account provokes a mix of bewilderment and tenderness. The Umbrian chronicler in fact tells us that Francis, in search of his interlocutor, the Sultan Malik al-Kamil, "before reaching him suffered much insult and harm, and not knowing their language he cried out among the beatings: *Soldan, Soldan*. And so he was led by him and was honorably received and treated very humanely in his illness" (*Jordan* 10). Without any interpreter, without any mediation, he threw himself into the fray with determination. No striking gesture made by his hero is revealed by Giordano's story, no heavenly sign comes to steal him from the hands of his adversaries. So it is difficult to think that we are faced with an invention or re-elaboration by the chronicler. The man of God appeared strong only in his weakness, a fact that also highlighted the magnanimity of the sultan.

Some time later, Giacomo da Vitry spoke again of that meeting, substantially confirming his earlier version and, in some way, Giordano's account: "We have seen the founder and master of this order," he wrote. "He was so moved by spiritual fervor and exhilaration that, after he reached the army of Christians before Damietta in Egypt, he boldly set out for the camp of the Sultan of Egypt, fortified only with the shield of faith" (*VitryHoc* 14: *FF* 2227).

Basically, the expedition resulted in nothing concrete. Yet that voyage, which may seem reckless to human reason, produced an "encounter" whose lesson is still thought-provoking. The one — Francis — unaware and lacking everything, went to the opposing camp not by using the force of arms, but "equipped only with the shield of faith." The other — Sultan Malik al-Kamil — welcomed him "honorably" and cared for him "very humanly in his illness." In time of war, they were able to listen to each other, making it possible for a brief fragment of time for the swords to be placed in the scabbard. Neither of them abdicated their faith, but that difference — though profound — did not prevent the encounter, nor was the possibility of a frank exchange denied, an exchange which lasted "for a few days."

Anything and everything has been said and written about Francis, to the point of spreading — in the common vernacular — an image which in many ways does not correspond to the truth. It is a different Francis each time, according to different needs and fashions, one who ends up having little in common with the flesh and blood man whom Thomas of Celano described as being "of medium height, closer to short," and, "because he was very humble, he showed meekness to all people, and duly adapted himself to the behavior of all" (*1Cel* 83: *FF* 465), who loved Christ above all else and from whom nothing and no one could separate him.

There is no need, however, to force the sources to assert his rejection of a logic based on a "class of religions." In this sense, his "encounter" with Sultan Malik al-Kamil still surprises us, revealing extraordinary humanity, ability to listen, understanding, and mercy on the part of both protagonists. Whereas the style of presence proposed in Chapter XVI of the *Regula Non Bullata* reveals all its extraordinary relevance. And I believe that it was precisely this event, together with the teachings that came out of it, which was one of the reasons that led John Paul II to elect the city of Assisi as the venue for prayer gatherings for peace.

Eight centuries after those events, we must recognize that this is still a prophecy for the future, a prophecy directed, in the first place, to all the children of Abraham — Jews, Christians, and Muslims — as well as all believers in God. It is a way that shuns cheap irenicism and demands mutual respect, acceptance, knowledge of the other; a way that seeks the truth through confrontation and dialogue, abdicating all forms of violence.

When Francis Predicted the Earthquake

Thomas of Eccleston, who died shortly after 1259, in his work on the settlement of the first Friars Minor in England (*De adventu fratrum Minorum in Angliam*), left us an extraordinary document of the life and habits of the friars, who arrived across the Channel in 1224. Among other things, Thomas recounts the memories of Brother Martin de Barton, "who was found worthy frequently to see the blessed Brother Francis" (*Eccleston* 166–67: *FF* 2460).

Among these appears the following:

> Another brother was found unhurt who was praying in a church at Brixen [Brescia] on Christmas Day when there came a great earthquake, so that the stones gave way and the church fell. This earthquake had been predicted by Saint Francis, and in a letter written chiefly in the Latin tongue he had caused it to be announced by the brethren in all the schools of Bologna. It hap-

pened before the war of the Emperor Frederic and continued for forty days, so that every mountain in Lombardy [by "Lombardy" the writer meant more or less all of northern Italy] was shaken.[1]

What credit can we give to this famous testimony, often cited by historians, if we focus more on the judgment on Francis's literary abilities than on the fact itself? Let us begin by saying that it is precisely the reference to Francis's false Latin that offers an element in favor of this account. Indeed, why should the reporter have invented such news? In other words, what interest could he derive from it? In reality, the Franciscan theologians and biographers of the saint try not to focus so much on the fact that Francis had defined himself, on more than one occasion, as ignorant and illiterate. By the middle of the thirteenth century, the order was widespread and Franciscan teachers held the most important university professorships. The founder's ignorance had become an inconvenient subject.

There is no doubt, then, that a tremendous earthquake shook the north of Italy on Christmas Day, 1222. The event was witnessed by too many chroniclers to question it. Salimbene da Parma, verbose as is his custom, does not lack — even on this occasion — picturesque details. "On the day of the Lord's Birth [1222], there was a great earthquake in the city of Reggio, while Bishop Nicola of Reggio was preaching in the cathedral of Saint Mary. This earthquake affected the whole of Lombardy and Tuscany, but it was called the Brescia earthquake, because its epicenter was there, and the citizens lived in tents outside the city, so as not to feel the buildings fall on them" (*Salimbene* 2: *FF* 2579).

The chronicler's account does not stop there, since it also adds personal references. "My mother used to remind me that during that great earthquake I was still a child in the cradle, and she took my two sisters (who were little) under her arm and, abandoning me in the cradle, sheltered in the house of her relatives. She feared that the baptistery would fall on her, because my house was near it. That is why I did not have excessive love for her, because she should have worried more about me, who was a male, but she replied that it was easier to bring the two sisters because they were older" (ibid.).

But not only that. Some preachers mentioned this forecast of the earthquake by Francis even before Thomas of Eccleston wrote his work. Among the sermons of John of La Rochelle (d. 1245) there is one that takes its cue from the famous biblical verse *Creavit Deus hominem ad imaginem et similitudinem suam* (God created man in his image and likeness), published in 1979 by Jacques-Guy Bougerol.[2] Although in this edition of the text — which also speaks of the foreknowledge of Francis — contains no mention of the earthquake, in years closer to us it has been published again by Jean Désiré Rasolofoarimanana, who found a version with many variations in a Latin codex preserved in Munich. It is, in fact, possible that the same sermon was transcribed by two different witnesses, thus presenting a considerable number of variations.

Now, the version preserved in the Munich manuscript states that Francis "was conformed to the Son in the foreknowledge of future things, since he announced an earthquake to the students early on and foretold the papacy to Pope Gregory [IX]."[3] A few years later, the same sermon would be taken as a model by an anonymous cardinal. The text pronounced by the cardinal was first published among the sermons of Bonaventure, in Volume IX of the *Opera omnia*, but, as Ignatius Brady has shown,[4] it cannot be from the Seraphic Doctor. The sermon published by the Quaracchi Fathers also contains a reference to the earthquake: Saint Francis, it is said, "predicted the precise day and time of an earthquake that should have occurred, and so happened, as he had predicted." The anonymous cardinal (Odo of Châteauroux?) thus took as his model a text close to the one transmitted to us by the Munich manuscript.

It is certain, then, that the news of an earthquake forecast by Francis circulated among the friars independently of the memories of Brother Martin of Barton, and so also the fact that the saint had the announcement made publicly to the students. And it is also certain that in 1222 Francis was in Bologna, certainly at mid-August. Thomas of Split, archdeacon and then bishop of his city, who in his youth had completed his intellectual training in the city of Felsina, in one of the most famous *Studia* of Europe, left us a colorful memory of it: "In that same year [1222]," he writes, on the feast of the Assumption of the Mother of God, finding myself at the Studium of Bologna, I saw Saint Francis preaching in the square in front of the town hall, where, one can say, almost the whole city had come together. ... All the substance of his words was aimed at extinguishing enmities and laying the foundations of new peace accords. He wore a filthy habit; his appearance was wretched, his face was without beauty. Yet God gave his words such effectiveness that many noble families, among whom the irreducible fury of inveterate enmities had burst to the point of shedding so much blood, were bent to councils of peace. The reverence and devotion of the crowd was very great, to the point that men and women threw themselves en masse at him, eager to touch at least the fringes of his tunic or to take a shred of his clothes.[5]

Of course, between the Assumption and Christmas there are more than four months, and in that period many things can happen. We don't know how long Francis stayed in Bologna, and in any case there are more clues that lead us to believe the story (at least in its substance) than not. It is difficult to know what happened in detail, and we do not know the reaction of those concerned, but it is not ludicrous to believe that Francis sent a serious warning to the Bolognese of that terrible event.

The Wound

Constitution 13 of the Fourth Lateran Council established that anyone who, from then on, wished to "convert" to religious life should embrace an "already approved rule." Francis of Assisi, however, with the drafting and, therefore, with the pontifical confirmation of his Rule, asked and eventually obtained a derogation from the decisions of the council. Much thought has been given to Francis's relations with the Roman See, especially with Cardinal Ugo of Ostia, but it is necessary to dig even deeper into the matter. Brother Leo testifies that during the famous Chapter of Mats (in all probability on Pentecost 1223), some friars intervened with Cardinal Ugo to persuade Francis to follow their advice and to assume one of the great rules already approved as their point of reference. Francis listened to the cardinal's exhortation, then took him by the hand and led him to the friars gathered in Chapter. To them he addressed a vibrant speech, reaffirming his unwillingness to make any decision that might in any way distort his religious intuition and aiming harsh words to those who let themselves be guided by their own "knowledge and wisdom." "Then the Cardinal was amazed and answered nothing, and all the friars were pervaded by fear" (*CAs* 18: *FF* 1564).

There is nothing to suggest that the initiative came from the cardinal. The friars who questioned him did not in fact ask for anything improper. On the contrary, they were acting in the spirit of the council's decisions. Could the cardinal, in the face of such a petition, offer a rejection, which would inevitably end up putting himself against the letter and the spirit of that council?

It was Francis who wanted to follow an uphill path to the end. In the end, only one reaction was possible for the cardinal, a reaction worthy of a fine and consummate diplomat such as Ugo of Ostia: to marvel and keep quiet. He thus decided to go down the riskiest path, that is, to collaborate in the drafting of the text that Francis wanted to present for pontifical approval, and to assist him and his brothers in the arduous journey toward that approval.

That risky decision, which in fact constituted a dangerous precedent for the Roman Curia, was made possible thanks to a juridical fiction, of which everyone was aware. The powerful and capable mediation of the Cardinal of Ostia made it possible to achieve the goal. It is understood that Ugo himself had to overcome considerable difficulties and opposition, to which, he could, however, oppose not only his juridical ability, but all the weight of his own authority. We will never know what happened in the months preceding pontifical approval. It is certain that Honorius III, in the *dispositio* of *Solet annuere*, the letter of November 29, 1223, in which he confirmed the Franciscan Rule, ended up affirming what he had avoided in previous letters:

> We confirm with Our Apostolic Authority, and by these words ratify, the Rule of your Order, herein outlined and approved by Our predecessor, Pope Innocent of happy memory. (*FF* 73a)

Honorius III therefore distinguished the *approbatio* from the *confirma*, attributing to himself only the latter and assigning the first, the *approbatio*, to his predecessor Innocent III. Ugo of Ostia could not and did not want to renounce the contribution of the new religious family. Faced with the determination of Francis, the cardinal preferred to endorse the one he, in any case, considered a man of God and support him in his request, even if in doing so Ugo of Ostia ended up going against his own views and the style he had previously adopted. But the stakes were too high and he did not want to risk it, nor could he afford to.

A few years later the same cardinal, who had now become Pope Gregory IX, was in a situation of evident difficulty for the Church. He bet decisively on the new mendicant orders, whose members would be progressively characterized by him as laborers of the eleventh hour. The wound inflicted on Lateran IV with Honorius III's confirmation of the Franciscan Rule had in the end its *raison d'être*.

The Poor King

It is a well-established conviction that it was Saint Francis who invented the Christmas creche in the celebration he held in Greccio in 1223. Was this really the case? And if not, what is the relationship between the Saint of Assisi and this beautiful Christmas tradition, which should be encouraged more and more?

Let us first of all summarize the facts. Francis arranged to celebrate the Eucharist worthily at Greccio on that solemn day. With the help of a man from the district, named Giovanni, he had straw put into a manger and even had an ox and an ass procured, so that it might be visible to all, with "the eyes of the body," how the child Jesus was born in Bethlehem, devoid of everything necessary for an infant. Giovanni prepared everything according to Francis's instructions. In that most solemn circumstance, the people rushed en masse carrying candles, and after meditating on the grandeur of the mystery, visually re-presented thanks to the scene set up by Francis, the altar was prepared on the manger and the Eucharist was celebrated. Francis, the deacon, intoned the Gospel and preached to the people, speaking with much emotion of that great mystery. After the celebration, all returned to their homes full of joy. This, in essence, is the account of Thomas of Celano, who was the first to narrate the episode in his *Life of Blessed Francis*, written between 1228 and 1229 (*1Cel* 84–86: *FF* 466–470).

From Thomas's account, it does not appear that Francis had any thought of staging a Christmas crib as we understand it today, a pure representation of a mystery of faith. Rather, he wanted to re-create the conditions for a real encounter with the mystery of the Lord's incarnation. There was no Child in the manger (nor was there anyone playing the roles of Joseph and Mary), but on that very manger the Eucharistic sacrifice was celebrated, because for Francis both realities — the Eucharist and the Incarnation — referred to the same basic choice, the choice of a God who humbles himself, who empties himself of his divine prerogatives, for the salvation of man.

Francis's thought is sufficiently clear in this regard, and is in tune with that of many other spiritual authors of the time. "Behold, each day he humbles himself," he writes in *Admonition I*, "as when he came from the royal throne into the Virgin's womb; each day he himself comes to us, appearing humbly; each day he comes down from the bosom of the Father upon the altar in the hands of a priest" (*Adm*, 16-18: *FF* 144). The Eucharist therefore perpetuates the Incarnation of Christ in history and, at the same time, demands that — like Christ — we know how to expropriate ourselves of everything, without keeping any part of us for ourselves. Francis cried it out loud in a lyrical passage from the *Letter to the Entire Order*:

> Let everyone be struck with fear, let the whole world tremble, and let the heavens exult when Christ, the Son of the living God, is present on the altar in the hands of a priest! O wonderful loftiness and stupendous dignity! O sublime humility! O humble sublimity! The Lord of the universe, God and the Son of God, so humbles himself that for our salvation he hides himself under an ordinary piece of bread! Brothers, look at the humility of God, and *pour out your hearts before him*! Humble yourselves that you may be exalted by him! Hold back nothing of yourselves for

yourselves, that he who gives himself totally to you may receive you totally![1]

In short, to dispossess oneself of everything, even of every expectation of others. On Christmas, 1223 Francis wished to recall this reality once again, presenting it visually to the inhabitants of Greccio and the nearby countryside.

It is appropriate to dwell on what Thomas says about the contents and methods of Francis's preaching. According to the hagiographer, that night the saint preached about the birth of the poor King and about Bethlehem, a small town. Therefore, the fulcrum of Francis's sermon on that holy night was aimed at contemplating the ways the Son of God chose for his entry into the history of humankind. The King was a poor king, the city in which he was born was a small city. This is undoubtedly a theme that returns to Francis's meditation and his proposal for a Christian life.

The hagiographer's notes on the details of that preaching are very interesting. Thomas affirms, in fact, that when Francis pronounced the word "Bethlehem," he did so by filling his mouth with tender affection and producing (obviously with the repetition of the first "e") a sound similar to the bleating of a sheep, and every time he said "child of Bethlehem" or "Jesus," he licked his lips and swallowed, almost as if to taste the sweetness of those words. Among hagiographers, Thomas, moreover, is the one who best informs us of the way in which Francis used all the resources of his body and voice to communicate his feelings, to the point of affirming that he had made his whole body into a tongue (*1Cel* 97: *FF* 488).

The Lord, therefore, was born once again, humble and poor as in Bethlehem, and asked men to follow in his footsteps. The mystery of the Incarnation and the Eucharistic Sacrifice, firmly united in the celebration desired by Francis (it is important to reiterate that the Eucharist was celebrated on the manger he had specially prepared), attested to an irrevocable choice on the part of the Son of God. Among other things, Thomas of Celano expressly says that "the humility of the Incarnation and the charity of the passion" of Jesus Christ occupied Francis's memory so much that he wished to think of nothing else. It is worth repeating:

Francis did not want to re-create a creche! There was no child in that manger, and Thomas himself takes care to explain the meaning of the vision of one of those present, a man — he specifies — of admirable virtue. The man had seen that in the manger lay a lifeless child, who, however, as Francis approached, had awakened from his deep torpor. This vision, Thomas clarifies, was not in contradiction to the reality of things, since, through his servant Francis, the child Jesus had awakened again in the hearts of many who had forgotten him.

How, then, can we justify the persistence of a misunderstanding that sees in the event of Greccio the first creche in history and in Francis the inventor of this pious tradition? It is, in reality, a completely modern misrepresentation. That is to say, there is no trace of it in the Middle Ages, as is clearly shown by the fact that in order to have an explicit affirmation of it, we have to wait until 1581, for Juan Francisco Nuño, a Spanish Franciscan who lived at the monastery of Aracoeli. It is true, nevertheless, that the night at Greccio exerted a profound influence on the later spread of the Christmas crib. One thinks, moreover, of what an extraordinary instrument of catechesis it ended up being in the controversy against the Cathar heresy, which denied the reality of the Incarnation and the humanity of Christ.

Yet how much deeper and more demanding was the message launched by Francis at Christmas, 1223: a message that was an invitation to accept the proposal of Jesus and to follow in his footsteps, in humility, in poverty, in the total expropriation of oneself, which he did with determination and strength, until the end.

That Blank Space without Notes

For his long-awaited encyclical on the environment, Pope Francis drew inspiration from the *Canticle of the Sun*, thus tying the document to the saint from whom he took his name. For those verses, Francis of Assisi had also composed the music, which unfortunately is lost. In the ms. *Assisano* No. 338, folio 33r, there was, in fact, an initial space where they should have marked the musical notations, which, unfortunately, remained blank!

This manuscript is also the oldest documentary evidence of the *Canticle*, because the part of the codex in which it was transcribed dates back to the 1240s: a relic, therefore, of the highest value. The column that introduces the text reads: "The praises of the creatures that the blessed Francis composed in praise and honor of God when he was sick at San Damiano." Francis therefore wrote them while he was ill. Scrolling through the verses, one is almost led to think of gardens full of flowers and green grass, gushing fountains and chirping birds; those *Laudes* were instead written in a particularly difficult moment.

In fact, the detailed testimony of the companions of the saint allows us to certify that Francis composed them at different moments, even far apart from one another.

In the first months of 1225, he stayed at San Damiano for more than fifty days, in the grip of atrocious suffering. One night, he could not take it anymore and invoked the help of the Lord, who answered him in spirit, "Brother, be glad and rejoice in your illnesses and troubles" (*CAs* 83: *FF* 1614). The following morning, he began to compose the *Canticle of Brother Sun*. That poem, which over the centuries has given peace and consolation to millions and millions of people was born in a moment of pain, an echo of a soul pacified in its depths and therefore capable of inviting all creatures to the praise of God.

The text was completed and then perfected over time. In fact, while Francis was still ill in San Damiano, a quarrel broke out between the bishop and the *podestà* of Assisi. He therefore added the verse about forgiveness to the *Canticle* and sent two of his companions to sing it to the contenders, who, after listening to it, embraced (*CAs* 84: *FF* 1616).

The composition was finally completed at the very end of Francis's life. With full awareness he recognized the "moment." After the doctor had revealed his true state of health to him at his bedside, Francis began to praise the Lord: "Welcome, my Sister Death!" (*CAs* 100: *FF* 1638). In the same way, a companion spoke frankly to him; even at that moment, the man from Assisi did not fail to praise the Lord, so he had Friar Leo and Friar Angelo sing the *Canticle of the Sun* to him, and before the last verse, he inserted the praise of sister death (*CAs* 7: *FF* 1547).

Many aspects of Francis's personality have certainly been exaggerated, others detached from their context and cut off from their source of inspiration, or else entirely born from some opinion leader's imagination. In reality, the root of all his behavior lies in the relationship he was rebuilding with the God whom he had ignored for much of his life. When he finally arrived at the definitive choice to leave the world — that is, to abandon the values pursued by the world (which had also been his until the age of twenty-four) — to rediscover the goodness and fatherhood of God, everything acquired a different meaning. He saw the face of Christ in the poor, enemies became people to love, animals his little brothers, and creation revealed itself to his eyes as the sign of the Creator.

He then became convinced that not only human beings were called to the praise of God, but all creation. Creation in its entirety must therefore celebrate the glory of the Creator: men, animals, plants, wind, water and fire, stars in the heavens, and every other inanimate creature. It is only in this context that we can understand the *Canticle of the Sun* in its full and true light.

This is the strength of Francis's discourse: The whole of creation is called to praise the Lord, but above all, the human being, who is at its summit, because everything has been given to him so that he may use it and return it to the Creator. In other words, it is a return to the concept of restitution. Since God is the giver of all that is good, all goods must be returned to him. Created work must be brought back to him, because everything praises and speaks of him. To do violence to creation means, therefore, to do violence to God himself.

The real drama is that creatures serve the Lord much better than man, for while they obey the Creator, man easily turns away. These are concepts which Francis expresses effectively in the fifth of his admonitions:

> Consider, O human being, in what great excellence the Lord God has placed you, for he created and formed you to the image of his beloved Son according to the body and to his likeness according to the Spirit. And all creatures under heaven serve, know, and obey their Creator, each according to its own nature, better than you. (*Adm V*, 1–2: *FF* 153–154)

It is therefore impossible to understand Francis's disposition toward creation and animals outside a theocentric horizon — that is, without God and the obedience owed to him. Respect for the environment passes through respect for and obedience to the Creator. He was, in fact, well aware that God had created the universe as a garden and wanted man, redeemed by the Blood of Christ, to return to obedience, so as to regain the initial state of Eden. Obedience, the sister of charity, a virtue little loved at all times, asks man to adapt his plans to those of God. And obedience is due, as Carlo Paolazzi writes, "not only to the Father who is in heaven, but also to the plan of life which he has inscribed in the whole family of his creatures." This is perhaps "the most unexpected and unheeded message of the entire religious culture of the Christian West" (*FF*, 170, note 13).

Listen, Poor Ladies

One of the most interesting findings of the last fifty years has been the discovery of a text that Francis of Assisi addressed to Clare and the sisters who lived with her at the church of San Damiano in Assisi. In their recollections — transmitted quite faithfully in the *Assisi Compilation* — the Companions of Francis inform us that the saint, during the same time in which he composed the first and largest part of the *Canticle of the Sun*, also wrote "some holy words with chant [*verba cum cantu*] for the greater consolation of the Poor Ladies of the Monastery of San Damiano. He did this especially because he knew how much his illness troubled them. And since he was unable to console and visit them personally because of that illness, he wanted those words to be proclaimed to them by his companions" (*CAs* 85: *FF* 1617).

After being hidden, we can say, for centuries, that text came to light in 1976 by a whole series of happy circumstances. The novices of the Protomonastery of Assisi noticed surprising correspondences between what was reported of those "words with melody" in the *Assisi Compilation* and a text that in 1941 had already been published by Father

Leonardo Bello, found in two codices (one parchment, the other paper) preserved by the Poor Clares of Novaglie near Verona. The novices referred it to Sister Chiara Augusta Lainati, who obtained the text from her sisters in Novaglie and republished it in the summer of 1977 in the first edition of the *Fonti Francescane*. The news was also communicated to Father Giovanni Boccali, who went to Novaglie, where he was able to examine the codices and propose a first dating (the first decades of the fourteenth century for the parchment codex, early sixteenth century for the paper codex). Boccali judged the text of *Audite, poverelle* to be authentic, both because the parchment codex expressly attributed its authorship to Francis and because of the continuity that the language and content of the poetry maintained with the language and thought of the saint.

The often-lively discussion that took place in the following years (a lucid essay by Aldo Menichetti was decisive in this regard) ended up confirming the authenticity of that short text, which I now reproduce in its entirety:

> Listen, little poor ones called by the Lord, / who have come together from many parts and provinces. / Live always in truth, / that you may die in obedience. / Do not look at the life without, for that of the Spirit is better. / I beg you out of great love, to use with discernment / the alms the Lord gives you./ Those weighed down by sickness / and the others wearied because of them, / all of you: bear it in peace. / For you will sell this fatigue at a very high price / and each one will be crowned queen / in heaven with the Virgin Mary. (*FF* 263/1)

Less well known is the fact that the news reported by the Companions of Francis had already attracted the attention of Giulio Salvadori. The poet, in his youth, had been an acquaintance of D'Annunzio and in 1885, in Ascoli, had rediscovered faith in God. He was a passionate scholar of Saint Francis of Assisi and Franciscan sources, as well as a sincere friend of Paul Sabatier, with whom he shared serious research projects.

Gian Francesco Gamurrini (1835–1923), a well-known scholar of the archaeology and history of Arezzo, to whom Salvadori was linked by feelings of gratitude and friendship, believed he had discovered unpublished verses of Saint Francis in a codex he found in the National Library of Naples. Even before publishing them, he wanted to share the enthusiasm of the discovery with Giulio Salvadori, who at first agreed with the illustrious scholar, but later distanced himself, all the while maintaining a tone of great sensitivity and discretion. Salvadori wrote to Gamurrini on December 9, 1900: "On the other hand, if he [Saint Francis] admonished the Sisters of Saint Clare that, since the Lord had gathered them from many places to be one in holy poverty and holy obedience, so in these same virtues they should live and die; why would he not have admonished the Friars Minor in the same way?"[1]

The episode reported by the Companions had therefore not gone unnoticed by Salvadori. Many years later, he published his *Ricordi di san Francesco d'Assisi* ("Memories of Saint Francis of Assisi") (Florence 1926), in which he reported the testimony and then wrote,

> He who gathers here these Lauds wishes to provide an idea of the verses accompanied by song, and he notes that the virtues which shone in the mind of Francis as beauties and graces of the holy soul as sisters in the *Salutation of the Virtues* return in this exhortation directed to Saint Clare and the other Poor Ladies. He has tried to recompose it in verses similar to those of the *Canticle of the Sun*, using words of Saint Francis, or ones proper to his speech, but not of his dialect. And he asks forgiveness from the saint and from the readers for his presumption.[2]

Salvadori then gave his version of the text:

> I pray to you, my Ladies, that you humbly listen to me: / Since the Heavenly Father has gathered you into one / To follow in sweet penance his beloved Son, in holy Charity with holy obedience, / In holy Poverty with the holy humility; and since the Holy Spirit with these virtues has adorned you, / I pray to the Blessed Virgin Mary that she may keep you, / So that in them

you might live and die. / Of the things that are placed there at the table of the Lord / provide for your bodies with discretion: / And the Most High praise, bless and thank with pure joy in simplicity and charity. / And may the poor sick in their infirmity and the healthy who care for them with compassion on those who suffer, / Blessedly sustain each other in patience and peace! / They will be crowned by the Most High Lord.[3]

As we can see, Salvadori allowed himself to be influenced more by the *Salutation to the Virtues* and by the *Canticle of the Sun* than by the testimony of his companions, who described the content of that text by Francis with great precision. Despite their "infidelity," however, these verses convey the candor of a sincerely Franciscan soul, who made his poetic art a hymn of praise to God.

Saint Francis in Rieti

Hagiographic sources attest to the presence of Saint Francis in Rieti more than in other places closer to Assisi and more easily accessible for him. Although he had close ties of friendship in Rieti — as evidenced by his relationship with John of Greccio and the events of Christmas 1223 — his stay in the city is limited, however, to one specific circumstance. In the *Life* that Thomas of Celano wrote during 1228-1229, it is said that Francis was oppressed by a progressive blindness. This blindness was the result of a very painful disease he had contracted in foreign lands 1219-1220, and which granted him no respite. He therefore went to Rieti, where there was an expert (*peritissimus*) ophthalmologist. It is, however, very difficult to identify him with *maestro* Nicola, a doctor from Rieti, of whom Angelo Sacchetti Sassetti found evidence in local archives: An expert of his renown would not have remained in Rieti, but would certainly have practiced in a larger city. Very probably — as Sacchetti Sassetti himself proposed — such a surgeon had to be with the papal court.[1]

"When he arrived there," reports Thomas, "[he] was received kindly and respectfully by the whole Roman Curia, which was then staying in that city. He was especially well received by Lord Hugolino, the bishop of Ostia" (*1Cel* 99: *FF* 492). We know that the Curia lived in Rieti from June 1225 to January 1226. Thomas's account coincides with that of the Companions of Francis, who in 1246 attested that he left Assisi "when the season conducive to healing of the eyes arrived." "Because he could not look at the light of day because of the great pain caused by his eye disease," they specify again on this occasion, "he was wearing on his head a large capuche the brothers had made for him, with a piece of wool and linen cloth sewn to the capuche, covering his eyes" (*CAs* 86: *FF* 1618). The same companions led him on horseback to Fontecolombo. At first Francis went to be with his friars, then he presented himself to Honorius III and the Curia.

Various details of his stay in the city come to us from the memories of his companions. It is they who reveal that, during his illness, Francis "was spending a few days in the bishop's palace in Rieti" (*CAs* 95: *FF* 1631). At the same time, a cleric named Gideon — in the hagiographic sources commonly characterized as worldly and full of vice — suffered from painful problems with his kidneys. The Chapter Archive of Rieti is able to attest to his existence between 1201 and 1236. One day, the sick man had himself brought to Francis, who admonished him for his licentious life, which was probably well known. He then marked him with the Sign of the Cross and entrusted him to the grace of God, warning him, however, not to return to his sin, should the Lord heal him, since he would receive a more serious condemnation. We know how it all ended. Gideon recovered, but he did not stop sinning, thus incurring a severe punishment. He lost his life — alone — in the collapse of a house.

What is important to highlight, however, is that — once again — the documentary sources come to validate the hagiographic memory, because the story of the Companions of the saint and the archival testimonies coincide on the name and the reputation of the cleric. The same can be said of Teobaldo Saraceno, in whose room Francis stayed for a few days (*CAs* 66: *FF* 1594). Sacchetti Sassetti also found traces of him in a document of the Chapter Archive, which identifies him as a canon from Rieti and shows him present at the drafting of a deed on July 10, 1220.[2] It was in the room of this canon that Francis asked one of his companions to entertain him with the sound of a zither. The friar refused, embarrassed at what people might have thought. It was therefore an angel with a zither who consoled Francis for a long time in the night.

These temporary residences clearly show that at the time the friars did not yet have a suitable place in Rieti to host Francis, weak as he was. He ended up staying for some time at the church of San Fabiano, which the Companions, in their memories, located outside the city. It was a settlement that should not be confused with the shrine of Santa Maria della Foresta, but instead was a church that a 1027 map from the Abbey of Farfa located outside of what in modern times was called Porta Aringo (*foris pontem civitatis*), near which the Poor Clares had established a monastery in 1289. Now, the presence of Francis brought that church outside the gates to the center of attention. It was cared for by a poor priest who owned a small vineyard right next to the house where the sick Francis was staying, which ended up being ruined by the continual arrival of cardinals and church dignitaries coming to visit him. The complaints of the priest, powerless in the face of the disruptions and plundering of all those passers-by, however, were answered by the reassurance of Francis, who prophesied an abundant harvest, as indeed happened (*CAs* 67: *FF* 1595).

The stories of the Companions are of an extraordinary narrative freshness. Thanks to them, we also know the story of an old lady from Machilone (today's Posta), so poor that her doctor himself was forced to give her food. When he informed Francis of her situation, he was so saddened that he convinced one of the friars with him to give the poor woman a cloak and twelve loaves. The gesture appeared incomprehensible to the woman, who, at first, considered herself the butt of a joke, but later, seeing that the friar "had spoken the truth, she accepted everything with trembling and her heart filled with joy. Then, fearful that he would take it back, she secretly got up during the night and joyfully returned to her home" (*CAs* 89: *FF* 1625).

Thomas of Celano also provides other episodes in the *Memoriale* (better known, though improperly, as the *Vita seconda*), which provides clear evidence of a sojourn that was anything but short, and left an imprint on the city of Rieti. Can this same memory still be able to produce fruits today?

The Little Plant of Brother Francis

Expanding and personalizing what was said in the *Regula Bullata* of the Friars Minor, Clare of Assisi defined herself as "handmaid of Christ and the little plant of the most blessed Father Francis" (*RsC* I, 3: *FF* 2751). Francis's little plant! The image is well known, as it is used by Clare especially in works written in her last years of life. In fact, it returns in the *Blessing* (v. 6: *FF* 2855) and in that much discussed text which is the *Testament* (vv. 37, 49: *FF* 2838, 2842), on whose authenticity, however, there is by now an almost general consensus.

What is less known, however, is the fact that, although she made abundant use of it, it was not Clare who first coined this term. In fact, the first to use it was Thomas of Celano in his *Life of Blessed Francis*, completed immediately after the canonization of the man from Assisi.

In the last chapter of Part Two, Thomas tells of Clare and her sisters weeping over the lifeless body of Francis:

They arrived, says Thomas,

at the place where he first planted [*plantavit*] the religion and the Order of the consecrated virgins and Poor Ladies. They laid him out in the church of San Damiano, home to those daughters he gained for the Lord. The small window was opened, the one used by these servants of Christ at the appointed time to receive the Sacrament of the Lord's Body. The coffin was also opened: in it lay hidden the treasure of supercelestial powers; in it he who had carried many was now carried by a few. The Lady Clare! Clearly a woman of true brilliance and holiness, the first mother of all the others, the first plant of that holy Order: she comes with her daughters to see the father who would never again speak to them or return to them, as he was quickly going away.[1]

It was thus Thomas who first made use of this similarity, which was destined to have an extraordinary fortune over time. Francis planted [*plantavit*] the order of the poor ladies, of whom Clare was the first plant [*prima planta*]. Her words were then taken up by Julian of Speyer and appeared again in the text of the *Umbrian Legend* (written 1237–1239).

Years later, the Companions of Francis would use the same image and apply it to different subjects. From Greccio, some of them — Leo, Rufinus, and Angel — addressed a series of recollections to the Minister General Crescenzio da Iesi, together with a letter dated August 11, 1246. They contain an extraordinary portrait of Clare, described as the "first little plant [*plantula*] of the order of the sisters, abbess of the Poor Sisters of the monastery of San Damiano of Assisi, emulating Saint Francis in always preserving the poverty of the Son of God" (*CAs* 13: *FF* 1558). Furthermore, the Companions reported that the simile of the little plant was used in several circumstances by Francis himself. According to their testimony, the saint wanted a group of friars of holy life to always live at the Portiuncula so that the place could remain as a "mirror and a good example for the entire religion" and be a "candelabra before the throne of God and before the blessed Virgin," so that the Lord would have mercy on the defects and sins of the brothers and preserve and protect "this religion, his little plant" (*CAs* 56: *FF* 1578). According to his companions, Francis therefore considered the Order of Friars Minor a "little plant" of the Lord.

All the material found in the investigation promoted by Crescenzio da Iesi was given to Thomas of Celano, who was asked to fill in the gaps found in the *Vita* he himself had written almost twenty years earlier. The hagiographer thus completed the *Memoriale*, a work in which the title of "little plant" is also attributed to Bernard of Quintavalle. It is said of him that he was, after the saint, "the first small sprout of the Order of Lesser Ones" (*2Cel* 109: *FF* 696). Both Bernard and Clare and the Order of the Poor Sisters were therefore little seedlings of the man from Assisi. Thomas and the Companions of Francis did not seem to have any uncertainties in this regard.

On August 11, 1253, Clare died at San Damiano. Two years later, she was canonized by Alexander IV in Anagni, in all probability on August 15. In the letter of canonization *Clara claris praeclara*, a real "vita" of the new saint, the pontiff also presented Clare as a plant and her order as a plantation, but neither appears any longer as a creation of Francis. In Alexander's letter it is Ortolana and Clare herself who take center stage. The statements in the letter of canonization would be taken up again, a few years later, in the *Legend of Saint Clare the Virgin*, also written during the pontificate of Alexander IV (therefore, between 1255 and 1261).

The writings of Clare and those of Thomas of Celano have remained, in reality, unknown to the general public for many centuries, and with them also the image of the "little plant" used by the saint of Assisi. Between the end of the nineteenth century and the first years of the following century, they came back to the fore, also bringing back into vogue that image which, however, was not created by Clare or used exclusively for her.

It remains to be seen who originated this allegory. Can we attribute it to Francis? In part, yes, in the sense that the image of the little plant can probably be traced back to him, although it is difficult to think that he would consider himself to be the author of the plantation. Ultimately, it is credible that Francis defined the Order of Minors as a seedling of the Lord and could also have called Bernard and Clare such, since he was convinced that the author of his own conversion, and of what followed was God. Clare and her sisters, Bernard and the others, for their part, could instead consider themselves Francis's seedlings, as in fact Clare did (and perhaps Bernard too, but we do not have his writings or words of this kind attributed to him).

In the light of what the sources tell us, we can thus believe that Francis used the metaphor of the little plant for Bernard, Clare, and the Order of Minors, speaking of them as God's little plants. It was then the others, Clare, the Companions of Francis, and the Franciscan hagiographers, who recognized the importance the saint had in their journey of conversion and life, and therefore who recognized themselves — without reservation — as his little plants, since he had been for them (as Clare said with particular force) founder and planter (*TestsC* 48: *FF* 2842), pillar, support, and only consolation after God (*TestsC* 38: *FF* 2838).

Beware of the Man, Not the Wolf

One of the most famous episodes in the life of Francis of Assisi is undoubtedly the story of the wolf of Gubbio, which the saint is said to have tamed and reconciled with the inhabitants of that city. In his writings, Francis speaks little ill about the wolf. In fact, he reveals a benevolent disposition toward it. He is not fearful of it, because he knows that he has nothing to fear, since he has never done any harm to brother wolf, as shown by an episode transmitted by a non-Franciscan source, to which credit must be given.

A monk from the second half of the thirteenth century left us some unpublished details at the end of the *Passion of San Verecondo*. The anonymous writer remembers that Francis had been hosted several times in the abbey (now Vallingegno, near Gubbio) and had always been welcomed there "with love."

Among other things, at the end he narrates an episode of infinite sensitivity:

Now Blessed Francis was wasted and weakened from frequently chastising his flesh, from nocturnal vigils, from praying and fasting, and thus quite unable to walk about; especially after he was marked with the wounds of our Savior he was not well enough to travel on foot, so he rode about on a little donkey. One evening when it was almost dark, Francis was on this donkey, traveling with his companion along the road to San Verecondo, his shoulders and upper arms covered with a rough sackcloth mantle, when some field laborers called out to him: "Brother Francis, stay with us here. Do not go any farther. Ferocious wolves are roaming about in this area. They will devour your little donkey and do you harm." Then Brother Francis replied: "I have done no injury to Brother Wolf, that he would attempt to harm our Brother Ass. Farewell, my sons, and fear God." And so Brother Francis continued on his way unharmed. This incident was reported to me by a farmer who was present at the time.[1]

It is not only the reference to the peasant who had been present and gave testimony that gives the story credibility. The very fact that the monastery is not assigned any role, no "positive" participation in the unfolding of events, already speaks in favor of the narrative's objectivity. Its reliability is also confirmed by the absence of any marvelous amplification (no miracle, no derogation of the laws of nature). The very words attributed to Francis, so paradoxical compared to the common sentiment, can hardly be considered the result of a reworking by the anonymous author. Everything, therefore, leads us to consider the episode as authentic, at least in its substance. Francis shows that he does not fear the wolf, not because he considers himself stronger and therefore able to keep him away, but because he judges the wolf's aggressiveness to be a response to the man's aggressiveness. If man did not do any harm (to animals and, we can suppose, to plants and to any other creature), he would not be assaulted, and the universe would return to the supreme harmony that had marked Adam's state.

This teaching is confirmed by the episode of the thieves of Montecasale, themselves wolves, ready to tear people apart, robbing and beating them. Francis advised the friars to approach them armed not with pitchforks and clubs, but with attitudes marked by exquisite charity, bringing food and wine. And they too, like the wolf of Gubbio, were tamed and moved to change their lives:

> Some entered religion, others embraced penance, promising in the hands of the brothers no longer to commit these evil deeds, but to live by the work of their hands. (*CAs* 115: *FF* 1669)

On the other hand, was it not written in the first Franciscan Rule:

> Whoever comes to [the brothers], friend or foe, thief or robber, let him be received with kindness. (*Rnb* VII, 14: *FF* 26)

It is also true that, despite his great openness to wolves — whether they had two or four legs — Francis was not at all shortsighted in the face of gratuitous violence and oppression. His natural goodness, his firm will not to build walls, was therefore not weakness in the face of evil, nor was it the fruit of harmful naivety.

These days there is a lot of discussion about welcoming others, and it is certainly not the first time that we have been faced with situations of need. In the last ten days of September 1971, faced with the millions of refugees who were fleeing Pakistan because of a civil war that consumed the country, Paul VI personally wrote an appeal, which *L'Osservatore Romano* only in recent years published in its entirety: "We now say," the great pontiff wrote on that occasion, "that the need is so great as to create an issue of justice; and which charity must, at least to some extent, resolve, according to its own method, with sacrifice and willingness."

The real risk is that, under the apparent motivation of good sense, we will all be driven to become — even without bad intentions — wolves. Didn't Plautus already say that man often becomes a wolf to his fellow man? *Homo homini lupus*. Commenting on the episode of the wolf of Gubbio, Father Primo Mazzolari said that the wolf is within each of us, even if there are two types of wolves. There is, in fact, "the wild wolf, the ravenous wolf," represented by the ravenous wolf of the story, which none of us has ever seen, and then there is "the polished, civilized wolf, who dresses well, the wolf in sheep's clothing, who is bothered by the wolf that comes from the forest."[2]

"Charity," wrote Paul VI, "must resolve [the issue] according to its own method." As if to say, the Gospel has its reasons that reason does not have! But the lessons of history also call for avoiding any kind of simplistic measures. In the fifth century, an empire that was on its last legs saw the barbarians descend from the north. Today, a Western civilization in decline is being pushed — even by cheap populisms — to recognize a new wave of "barbarians," this time rising from the south. At that earlier time, the fusion of various populations laid the foundations for a new civilization, that of the West. These two situations are distinct for many reasons, and we do not know how tomorrow will be, but the solution certainly will not come by building stockades.

Francis and the Workers of the Eleventh Hour

On October 4, 2013, Pope Francis went to Assisi. His visit was in some way reminiscent of the visit made centuries earlier (July 1228) by one of his illustrious predecessors, Gregory IX, in which he presided over the canonization of Francis, who had died two years earlier.

Francis's canonization had become a foregone conclusion. The sources help us to understand that the local authorities and ruling classes absolutely wanted him to remain within the walls of Assisi. Somewhat crudely, Thomas of Celano reports that this is what his own fellow citizens hoped (*1Cel* 105: *FF* 502). So in the last weeks of his life, Francis was closely guarded by the people of Assisi, who had every interest in keeping within their city the relics of a saint who would protect the community and also guarantee its economic prosperity (*CAs* 96, 99: *FF* 1632, 1637). The very decision to place Francis's remains in a temporary tomb and not in the cathedral leads us to conclude that ever since the death of the man from Assisi, not only the plan for his imminent elevation to sainthood, but also, in all probability, the idea of the construction of a church in his honor had taken shape.

The declaration of sainthood came two years later. Thomas of Celano informs us that the pontiff, who had fled from Rome following riots in the city, moved to Rieti. From there, on April 29, he addressed to all of Christendom the letter *Recolentes*, in which he sang the praise of the Friars Minor and gave Francis the title of blessed, announcing how it seemed "worthy and fitting" that, "out of the reverence toward the same father," "a particular church" would be built in which to house his body. The pope granted an indulgence of forty days to all those who would give alms for the accomplishment of this work (*FF* 2719). From Rieti, the pope then went to Spoleto and from there finally reached Assisi, where he began the *solemnis collatio*, summoning the cardinals on several occasions to complete all the established procedures and thus arrive at the official proclamation of Brother Francis's sainthood.

While the process of canonization was still in progress, the pope went to Perugia, where he attended to various matters. He then returned to Assisi to attend to the *negotium*. At the end of the labors, the sacred consistory was celebrated *in camera domini papae* (in the Lord Pope's chambers) in Perugia. This led to the canonization ceremony in Assisi, which Thomas of Celano narrates with detailed precision. His story is in fact so full of details that we can rightly grant him an eyewitness's license.

Indeed, the hagiographer tells that, after arriving at the place determined for the celebration, the cardinals, bishops, and abbots arranged themselves around the pope. Then priests and clerics, men and women religious, together with an immense crowd, rushed in. He accurately describes not only the different phases of the ceremony, but also the sparkle of the clothes of the prelates, adorned with filaments and golden buckles set with precious pearls.

Pope Gregory was the first to speak, he notes: After "proclaiming the praises of God in a resonant voice," he delivered a speech that began with a well-known passage from Scripture, "Like the morning star among the clouds, like the moon when it is full; like the sun shining upon the temple of the Most High, and like the rainbow gleaming in glorious clouds" (Sir 50:6–7). "Recalling [Francis's] way of life and speaking of his purity, he is drenched in tears." Following this, Cardinal Ottaviano degli Ubaldini gave a reading of the miracles of Francis, which were commented on, again with great emotion, by Cardinal Raniero Capocci. Everyone was moved to tears. Gregory IX then announced the inscription of Francis into the catalogue of saints, and the pope and the cardinals sang the *Te Deum*. Finally, the pontiff came down from his throne and "*enters the sanctuary to offer prayers and sacrifices*," kissed the tomb of the saint with great emotion, prayed with great intensity, and "celebrates the sacred mysteries" (*1Cel* 125–126: *FF* 538–542).

Shortly after that ceremony, it would seem, the pontiff also placed the first stone of the basilica to be built in honor of the new saint. We know this by his own explicit admission in the letter *Speravimus hactenus* (June 16, 1230) and as attested to by the hagiographic memory of the order. He then announced the great event to the world with the letter *Sicut phiale auraee*, and again with the letter *Mira circa nos*. This last letter — certainly more involved than the previous one — exerted a definite influence on Francis's hagiography, as attested by the clear connection that the text maintains with the oldest work of the whole corpus relative to Saint Francis of Assisi, the *Life of Blessed Francis* by Thomas of Celano.

The pontiff presented the entire earthly story of the new saint in a providential light:

> The Lord never ceases to protect the vineyard he planted with the gifts of his mercy, and even in the eleventh hour he sends workers who, by clearing the ground of weeds, thorns, and brambles, pruning the unnecessary shoots, allow it to produce sweet and delicious fruits, which will be stored up for eternity, after they have burned away the impiety and the charity that has cooled in the hearts of many. (*FF* 2720)

Twice the papal letter makes reference to the eleventh hour, with doubtless and significant allusion to the gospel parable of the workers sent by the master to his vineyard at different times of the day (Mt 20:1–16).

In a situation of evident difficulty for the Church, Gregory IX thus aimed decisively at the new mendicant orders, whose members were progressively characterized in his letters as workers of the eleventh hour. In the letter *Mira circa nos*, the pontiff thus made a choice of enormous significance for the Church. Albeit still in a prudent manner, he advanced the idea that it was precisely the new mendicant orders, and not the great monastic orders, which the Apostolic See had until then tasked with the most sensitive and important missions, that were the chosen militia for the battle that awaited the Church at such a crucial historical juncture: the end times and future judgment.

The pontiff therefore assigned to the mendicant orders a task of primary importance in his great plan. A key element of Francis's life thus became his preaching, rich in simplicity, but which had the power to heal and make fertile, like the water Ezekiel saw flowing from the Temple toward the East and which revived all that it touched (Ez 47:1–12). In this way, the pontiff offered the Order of Minors a clear model to inspire its actions to carry out the planned reform of the Church.

Like his predecessor, Pope Francis went to Assisi to pay homage to the saint who bears so much meaning and significance in the life of the Church, both past and present. Like his predecessor, he pronounced important words, worth meditating on.

The Magnet of Assisi

On December 12, 1818, after almost six centuries of oblivion, the mortal remains of Saint Francis of Assisi, until then inaccessible to all, were finally brought to light in the Basilica dedicated to his name. For safety reasons, the tomb had been dug into the rock, under the altar of the so-called lower Basilica, so that for centuries no one could come into direct contact with the stone sarcophagus containing the remains of the man from Assisi.

This lack of visibility was progressively overlaid with the image of Francis as *alter Christus*: The stigmata, the "final seal" (Dante, *Paradiso* XI, 107), made it possible for the saint to be assimilated to Christ crucified. Along the way, the idea of his resurrection also wound up taking shape. Bonaventure had written that the "most holy flesh" of Francis, "crucified together with his vices," transformed "into a new creature, showed to the eyes of all, through a unique privilege, the effigy of the passion of Christ and, through a never seen before miracle, anticipated the image of the Resurrection" (*LegM* XV, 1: *FF* 1246). The Spiritual Franciscans went further between the end of the thirteenth century and the beginning of the fourteenth, as Raoul Manselli clearly showed more than forty years ago. The Provençal author Pietro di Giovanni Olivi (d. 1298), in his *Commentary on the Apocalypse*, stated that he had received the confidence of a friar who was a close relation of Friar Leo, companion of Saint Francis. According to him, the man from Assisi, made similar to the crucified Christ, would also be so in resurrection, rising gloriously. A few years later (1305) the same things were also reported by Ubertino da Casale in the first draft of his monumental work, *The Tree of the Crucified Life of Jesus*, on the basis of the revelations collected by the friar from the Italian Marches, Corrado da Offida (*FF* 2097).

Later, in the fifteenth century, it was mainly the Observant Franciscan preachers who were responsible for spreading the idea of the incorrupt body of Saint Francis, to the point of producing an account that would only be proven false in 1818, precisely with the discovery of the sarcophagus containing the saint's remains. According to this extraordinary account, which takes on an initial written form with Giacomo Oddi da Perugia (d. 1478), author of *La Franceschina, overo Specchio de l'Ordine Minore* ("Mirror of the Friars Minor"), in 1476 Sixtus IV himself, together with a very small group of people, entered Francis's burial place one night. They found his body incorrupt and so beautiful "that he did not seem to be dead, but rather asleep."

The story, further perfected, was taken up in his *Chronicles* by the Portuguese friar Mark of Lisbon, then bishop of Porto. The bishop, immediately after the middle of the sixteenth century (the edition of the first part of this famous work is 1557), reproduced the text of a written report which narrated the inspection conducted in 1449 by Nicholas V. To the pope and to the small group that accompanied him — in this case more numerous than that of Sixtus IV — Francis no longer appeared almost asleep, but, with an incorrupt body standing upright, as if alive. The enormous dissemination of the Portuguese friar's *Chronicles* — soon translated into various languages — ensured the story an extraordinary fortune. It was taken up and reworked by several authors, Franciscans and non-Franciscans, even in subsequent centuries. But there were also critical voices, starting with the Bollandists, who entered into the conversation with all the weight of their authority. In the eighteenth century the debate became particularly heated and wound up entangled with the tensions between the Conventuals, custodians of the *Sacro Convento*, and the Observants, to whom the Portiuncula was entrusted. The latter asserted that the heart of Francis was preserved at the Portiuncula. They even went so far as to support the idea that the body of Francis, far from being kept lifelike and upright, was not even preserved in the basilica, but was transferred by the friars elsewhere. They shared this opinion with Flaminio Annibali da Latera, whose 1779 work, *How Uncertain It Is that the Body of the Seraphic Saint Francis Exists in Assisi in the Basilica of His Name*, was printed in Lausanne, under the cover of prudent anonymity.

Not all Observants, in truth, went so far. Indeed, the Observant historian Ireneo Affò openly disagreed with Annibali: "I cannot agree with the author of a booklet imprinted in 1779 with the date [sic] of Lausanne," he wrote in the *Vita di Frate Elia* ("Life of Brother Elijah"), published in Parma in 1783 (57). And since he did not believe in the incorruptibility of the body of Saint Francis, he hypothesized that in 1230, Elia arranged the translation of his body from the church of Saint George in a very circumspect way, precisely because he had found himself faced not with an incorrupt corpse — an unquestionable sign of holiness — but with a body "reduced to ashes and bones" (*Vita di Frate Elia*, 54). Moreover, in light of a whole series of ancient testimonies, Affò considered the idea that the remains of the saint had not been deposited in the Basilica to be unfounded.

These were the last great flames of an endless controversy. Shortly thereafter, the French Revolution came to announce not the end of the world — as was said then — but the end of a world. At the beginning of the nineteenth century, the Napoleonic suppressions would then fall with the force of a cyclone on the religious congregations, opening new scenarios. Finally, the discovery of Francis's tomb in 1818 wrote a final word, both on the myth of his presumed resurrection, and on the controversy about the real existence of his mortal remains in the Basilica of Assisi.

After two centuries, that same tomb has become the real magnet, the pulsating center of Assisi: an unequivocal sign of the presence of the one whose "wonderful life were better sung in Heaven's glory" (*Paradiso* XI, 95–96).

Blame the Tower of Babel

Commenting on the text of Mark 7:31–37, Pope Francis said that the teaching to be drawn from it is that

> God is not closed in on himself, but instead he opens himself and places himself in communication with humanity. ... But this Gospel speaks to us also about ourselves: Often we are drawn up and closed in on ourselves, and we create many inaccessible and inhospitable islands. Even the most basic human relationships can sometimes create realities incapable of reciprocal openness: the couple closed in, the family closed in, the group closed in, the parish closed in, the country closed in. And this is not from God! This is from us. This is our sin.[1]

Of course, the history of individuals and of peoples shows that it is not always easy to be open to the other, and that enmity and suspicion often prevail. But it is also true — and many recent examples from throughout Europe demonstrate this — that integration is possible and can prove to be a precious resource, today like yesterday. For this reason, I draw my inspiration from a thirteenth-century source, restricted to the European sphere, specifically to the Germanic world, but written by an Italian, Friar Jordan of Giano, who personally met Saint Francis and died in Germany shortly after 1262.

Jordan was the author of a precious *Chronicle*, which tells how, after 1217, the Friars Minor attempted their first missions across the Alps, in France, Spain, Germany, and Hungary (the dates he reported are not always certain). Their initial attempts were rather clumsy. The friars left hastily, without a precise plan and adequate preparation, unaware of the language and customs of the places where they would go. In France, they were asked if they were Albigensians and they "replied yes, not understanding what 'Albigensians' meant" (*Jordan* 4: *FF* 2326), or perhaps not understanding anything of what they were told. In Germany, however, the friars, "not knowing the language, were asked if they would like a food and lodging, and answered 'Ja.' So they were received by some good-naturedly. And noting that with this word 'ja' they were treated humanely, they decided to answer 'ja' to anything that was requested of them. For this reason it happened that, when asked if they were heretics who had come to contaminate Germany, precisely as Lombardy had been perverted, they answered 'ja' again" (*Jordan* 5: *FF* 2327). We easily can imagine the consequences.

A few years later, the friars showed that they had learned their lesson. Since their early ignorance of the German language had cause them some beatings, they did not repeat the mistake a second time. They placed at the head of the mission a German friar, Caesarius of Spire, who also gathered around him friars capable of acting as interpreters and able to preach both to priests and to common people.

Jordan is a very passionate chronicler who wins over the reader. He is succinct and very close to reality, but also capable of humor. In the art of storytelling he is equal to Salimbene da Parma — perhaps the most famous Franciscan chronicler of the thirteenth century — although much less mischievous and gossipy. His account of the sending of the friars to the second German mission (1221), in addition to revealing different aspects of the chronicler's character, offers interesting information on the atmosphere that reigned in the General Chapters and on the ways in which the order was governed.

From reading the *Chronicle,* Jordan emerges as a man with very little resolve, slow to decide on the choices to be made. He was an indecisive man, at least at the time he left for Germany, a land where not only did he not have to face martyrdom, but where he lived for more than forty years in positions of responsibility. He would later recount his experiences to the younger friars, teaching them that even ordinary men can become heroes in spite of themselves.

This indecisive man, however, was a spirited man, capable of displaying, at times, a complete shamelessness. An example of this that dates back to 1222, the year after his arrival in Germany, seems significant to me. Jordan was with Friar Abramo and Friar Costantino in Salzburg, their initial destination. Since they had not taken part in the Chapter held in Worms, the provincial minister, Caesarius of Spire, had two friars bring them letters (clearly letters of obedience) asking them to come to him. After they had started on their way, Jordan and his men came to a town and began to ask for food to quell their hunger. Yet, the tune was always the same:

> They heard the answer in German, *God berad,* which translates as "God help you," or rather, "May God provide for you." One of them, noting that they were not offered anything with that sentence, thought about it and said, "This *God berat* will be the death of us today." And going ahead of his brother friar, who was begging in German, he began to plead in Latin. But the Germans replied, "We don't understand Latin; speak to us in German!" And the friar, pronouncing in crippled German, said, *Nicht diudisch,* which means "No German." And he added in German, *Brot durch Got* ["Bread for God"]. His listeners answered, "It is extraordinary that you, speaking in German, claim not to know German." And they added, *"God berad."* This time the friar, smiling and happy in his heart, pretended not to understand what they said, and sat on a bench. Then a man and a woman looked at each other and, smiling at his goodness, gave

him bread, eggs, and milk. Seeing, therefore, that with such a useful fiction he could meet his and his brothers' needs, passed through twelve houses with this system, begging so much that it was enough for the seven brothers.[2]

It is evident that this brazen friar, who was capable of transforming his own worries into a powerful weapon, who made his weakness into his strength, was Jordan himself. He reveals that, in the short space of a year, the three friars who had begun the mission in Salzburg were joined by four others from that area, the same friars who during the course of the quest interacted with the people in German. Nevertheless, at that time the art of getting by was all Italian, and it was up to Jordan to make sure everyone was taken care of.

This episode, as well as the entire *Chronicle*, also shows that not all Germans were cruel — as Jordan judged before he met them — and that not all foreigners went to Germany to cause harm. The same can be said today: How many immigrants who knock at our doors in this climate of fear will turn out to be a precious resource for our countries tomorrow?

Saint Francis, the Most Italian of Saints

Francis of Assisi, "the holiest of Italians, the most Italian of the saints": Typing the phrase on any web search engine, you will notice that most of the time it is ascribed to Pius XII, who on June 18, 1939, proclaimed Saint Francis of Assisi and Saint Catherine of Siena the principal patrons of Italy. However, there is no lack of attributions to Pius XI or to "*Il Duce*," Benito Mussolini, as well as to many other lesser-known but no less significant figures. In reality, at least the first part of the saying dates back to Vincenzo Gioberti, who coined it in his most famous work, *Del primato morale e civile degli italiani* ("The Moral and Civil Primacy of the Italians" [1843]). In exalting the wisdom and greatness (even in human terms) of the Christian saints with respect to the pagan world, he revived in order to celebrate the "humble, yet beautiful and grand, simplicity, of affection and works" of Francis of Assisi "who is the most lovable, the most poetic, and the most Italian of our saints!"[1]

With this expression, the Abbot of Turin indissolubly linked the man from Assisi to the Italian genius, of whom he was the highest expression in the field of holiness. Later, such an interpretation became useful to Catholics in the new climate of postunification Italy, when, especially after 1870, they were presented by anticlerical publications as "bad" Italians. This patriotic reading of Francis then represented an opportunity to reaffirm their full right of citizenship as honest subjects and not enemies of the nation, citizens with equal dignity and not second-class citizens.

Meanwhile, the date of 1882 was approaching, the year in which the seventh centenary of the saint's birth was to be celebrated. In preparation for the event, Friar Ludovico da Casoria, the tireless apostle of charity, not only set about preparing a banquet for five thousand poor people in Naples on his feast day (October 4), but he also invited every Italian city to do the same. In the months preceding the momentous date, he therefore multiplied the number of letters so that his initiative would be accepted. To this end, in the one sent on August 3, 1882, without ever mentioning Gioberti, he expressly cited his definition of the saint of Assisi. "Who would be so hardhearted," he wrote on the occasion, "as to oppose spending one hundred or two hundred liras to cheer up the country with a table of 50 or 100 poor people in honor of Saint Francis, who was also called the most lovable and the most Italian saint!"[2]

Gioberti's description had therefore become deeply rooted. Inevitably, the 1882 centenary also produced a large number of new publications on Saint Francis. However, it was the Protestant pastor Paul Sabatier who contributed more than any other to placing the saint at the center of a broad and prolonged historiographical debate. At the end of November 1893 (even though the volume is dated 1894), Sabatier published his famous *Vie de saint François* ("Life of Saint Francis"), a work that immediately became a source of strong opposition, generating both enthusiastic acclaim and harsh criticism.

On October 3, 1902, in the hall of the *Circolo San Feliciano*, in Foligno, Italy, Monseigneur Michele Faloci Pulignani, one of the most active voices in the debates of those years, gave a lecture on Saint Francis of Assisi according to Sabatier. The occasion helped to rekindle the controversy, not so much with Sabatier as with Pulignani's detractors in the Catholic sphere, who accused him of "hyperconservatism." That first conference was followed by two other talks by the priest. In particular, on November 22, the confrontation seemed to take on a new tone. Faloci Pulignani spoke about "The Study of Saint Francis in Italy." In it, he reaffirmed the importance and the pre-eminence of Italian scholars, with accents that bordered on a still cautious patriotism, using expressions that seemed to echo many of Gioberti's utterances in his *Del primato*. At the time, the priest from Foligno had close contacts with many Roman circles, and I believe that it was precisely this speech that influenced the article published by Enrico Filiziani in the intransigent Catholic newspaper *La Vera Roma* ("The True Rome") on January 18, 1903, entitled "Per San Francesco d'Assisi (For Saint Francis of Assisi)." "No one should dare," disdainfully exclaimed the author, "to touch with an unworthy and cowardly brush one of the masterpieces of grace! Saint Francis remains, as reality shows us, the holiest of Italians, the most Italian of saints."[3] It was then that the slogan achieved its complete form, with which it would be handed down.

Then came the years of the "Great War," in which the image of the man from Assisi returned, dressed in a new patriotism. In this different context, Gabriele D'Annunzio undoubtedly played a leading role. In 1925, D'Annunzio had installed in the Vittoriale — his villa-mausoleum on the shores of Lake Garda — a statue of Saint Francis with a dagger hanging from the rope around his waist. The fact that this transformation was a perversion was evidenced by his notebooks from the air raid on Cattaro (today's Kotor).

On the night between October 4 and 5, 1917, D'Annunzio captained an aerial formation of fifteen bombers with which, after taking off from the Gioia del Colle airport, in the dark and with the help of compasses and stars to orient themselves, reached the Dalmatian coast and attacked the Austro-Hungarian fleet anchored at the Gulf of Kotor. On that occasion, the poet noted:

> The Seraphic One has purified the night. I say to my comrades, It is the night of Saint Francis, the most Italian of saints, the holiest of Italians. The Seraphic One is the patron saint of "overseas voyages." When he left from Ancona to go to the Holy Land, he

drew the line in the sea of our route through the air. But I tell you tonight he will make his hood into a wing and outstretch it with his cord.

Then begins the Franciscan litany of war.

For Brother Wind who will not oppose us, eia eia eia eia! Alalà!
For Brother Fire who will not burn us, eia eia eia eia! Alalà! For Sister Water who will not drown us, eia eia eia eia! Alalà! [4]

In this way the image of Saint Francis ended up becoming a tool for the exaltation of a crude nationalism. In the following years, this reference returned in an almost obsessive way, prompting Italians to look at the Saint of Assisi as the symbol of the rebirth of Italy, despite the tempering warning of Pius XI who published his encyclical *Rite expiatis* on the seventh centenary of the death of Francis (1226), and pointed out the risks of reading it through the lens of nationalism.

Unfortunately, the warning of Pius XI went largely unheeded. Francis of Assisi appeared to most people as the new herald of a civilization that, after overcoming the barriers erected by liberal governments, could look to the future with new eyes. And this new reality foreshadowed an increasingly patriotic reading of the figure of Saint Francis, aimed at blessing the new fascist course.

In any case, it is not true, as is currently stated, that Pius XII defined Francis as "the most Italian of the saints, the holiest of the Italians," since *Papa* Pacelli never made his own the slogan that had been so much in vogue in previous years.

In the meantime, an era was coming to an end. Shortly after the proclamation of Saint Francis as Patron Saint of Italy in 1939, war would invade the territory. That dramatic event, with the changes that followed, certainly did not allow Italians any kind of nationalist rhetoric, not even when it came to extolling their own saints.

Thus other scenarios opened up, in which the extraordinary figure of Francis of Assisi, like a seven-headed hydra, would offer new and different possibilities of interpretation. But this is another story.

An Inclusive Vision: Saint Francis according to Pope Francis

On March 13, 2013, from the periphery of the world, Jorge Mario Bergoglio ascended the throne of Peter. The fact that it would be a different, innovative pontificate was immediately clear, starting from the name assumed by the new pontiff, which signaled a bold choice of direction.[1]

BERGOGLIO'S READING AND ITS REPERCUSSIONS ON THE LIFE OF THE CHURCH

On March 16, 2013, in his first meeting with journalists a few days after the election, the pope clarified the reason for his decision. He specified that once the *quorum* for the papal election was reached, Cardinal Claudio Hummes, who was close to him, hugged him and said: "Do not forget the poor!"

"And those words came to me," said the Pope, leaning his right index finger on his temple. And he continued,

> the poor, the poor. Then, right away, thinking of the poor, I thought of Francis of Assisi. Then I thought of all the wars, as the votes were still being counted, till the end. Francis is also the man of peace. That is how the name came into my heart: Francis of Assisi. For me, he is the man of poverty, the man of peace, the man who loves and protects creation; these days we do not have a very good relationship with creation, do we? He is the man who gives us this spirit of peace, the poor man. ... How I would like a Church which is poor and for the poor!

In the immediate reading of Saint Francis that the Pope gave, he summed up his life experience in the signs of poverty, peace, and love for creation, wishing for greater attention to the poor on the part of the whole Church.

On other occasions, too, Francis stressed the importance of this aspect. July 24, 2013, in Rio de Janeiro, in the festive atmosphere of World Youth Day, he visited the *Saõ Francisco de Assis na Providencia* hospital, where he said that the young Francis abandoned "riches and comfort in order to become a poor man among the poor." On October 4, 2014, during the vigil of the opening of the Synod on the Family, he said, "Our listening and our discussion on the family, loved with the gaze of Christ, will become a providential occasion with which to renew — according to the example of St Francis — the Church and society. With the joy of the Gospel we will rediscover the way of a reconciled and merciful Church, poor and a friend of the poor."

In Rio de Janeiro (July 24, 2013), however, the Pope went deeper into his interpretation by associating Francis's choice of poverty with his embrace of the leper. It was precisely in that embrace, he said, where Francis's choice to become poor among the poor became concrete. "To embrace, to embrace — we all have to learn to embrace the one in need, as Saint Francis did." In fact, it was the lepers who made Francis (the saint) achieve the overturning of his own criteria that led to his conversion. In his *Testament*, Francis of Assisi defined going among the lepers as his chief moment of conversion, a reality he had previously avoided.[2]

"This means," wrote Raoul Manselli, "that the central moment of Francis's conversion" was "the passage from one human condition to another, the acceptance of one's insertion into marginality, his joining the excluded."[3] Francis therefore summarized his moment of conversion as a reversal of values. In the search for what he had previously avoided, in choosing a state of marginalization that could only lead to a deep following of Christ, he identified the essential nucleus of his religious proposal.

This gesture of Francis still appears in the words of the pope. Take for example his address to the new cardinals at the Consistory in February 2015:

> May we always have before us the image of Saint Francis who was unafraid to embrace the leper and to accept every kind of outcast. Truly, dear brothers, the Gospel of the marginalized is where our credibility is at stake, is discovered and is revealed!

Let us be frank: We are not yet used to such language, nor to seeing it used on such occasions, language that we should instead assimilate and make our own, along with the content it conveys.

FROM THE POVERTY OF CHRIST TO THE FLESH AND BLOOD POOR

Nor can it be said, as some would like to persuade us, that such a reading lends itself to a sociological reduction, endorsing a horizontal vision of religious experience, which instead had its roots in an intense faith experience. This would be false, because on the one hand there is the testimony of the sources, which clearly document the love of Francis for Christ and his brothers. On the other hand, there is the magisterium of Pope Francis, who keeps the two aspects of that experience united. The fact that the two aspects cannot be separated is shown first of all in the *Testament* of Francis. It clearly documents that the man from Assisi believed that the "Christian proposal" inspired by the Lord could be proposed again, even in the context of an institutionalized order. He even demanded that the friars — all of them — live by that model.[4] Giovanni

Miccoli is right, therefore, when he states that one cannot "reduce the 'evangelical life' proposed by Francis to a social choice," and reaffirms that "for Francis, only this type of social choice gives substance to his intention of following in Christ's footsteps."[5]

Now, those two aspects are united so as to be inseparable, because the suffering of real people (the lepers) enabled Francis to reach the crucified Christ and the crucified Christ enabled him to give meaning and significance to people's suffering.[6] The two are held firmly together by the pontiff who in his Message for the XXIX World Youth Day (January 21, 2014) wrote:

> Saint Francis of Assisi understood perfectly the secret of the Beatitude of the poor in spirit. Indeed, when Jesus spoke to him through the leper and from the crucifix, Francis recognized both God's grandeur and his own lowliness. In his prayer, the Poor Man of Assisi would spend hours asking the Lord: "Who are you?" "Who am I?" He renounced an affluent and carefree life in order to marry "Lady Poverty," to imitate Jesus and to follow the Gospel to the letter. Francis lived in imitation of Christ in his poverty and in love for the poor — for him the two were inextricably linked — like two sides of one coin.

We could discuss, if we really want to split hairs, the choice of referring to a late and uncertain text such as the *Considerations on the Stigmata*, where the marvelous aspects emerge more than the real,[7] when there are so many more certain texts available. But certainly one cannot doubt the overall correctness of Pope Francis's interpretation, especially when he speaks of Saint Francis's "imitation of Christ in his poverty and in love for the poor" as "two sides of one coin."

There are examples of this revealed in some of the pope's statements in his interview with the newspaper *La Stampa*, January 11, 2015. The journalists asked him, "Your words on the poor 'flesh of Christ' have struck many people. Does the accusation of 'pauperism' disturb you?" The pope then brought Saint Francis into play, recalling how, before his appearance on the horizon of history, there were already "pauperists."

But pauperism, he said, "is a caricature of the Gospel and of poverty itself. Instead, Saint Francis helped us to discover the profound link between poverty and the path of the Gospel. Jesus affirms that you cannot serve two masters, God and mammon. Is that pauperism? Jesus tells us the 'protocol' that will be used to judge us. It is what we read in chapter twenty-five of Matthew's Gospel."

THE PRIMACY OF THE EXPERIENCE OF FAITH

A few months after his election to the supreme pontificate, on October 4, 2013, the pope had the opportunity to offer a full presentation of the extraordinary personality of Francis of Assisi, on his first visit to Assisi. On that occasion, Pope Francis left a mark on the city of "his" saint,[8] even if, perhaps, not in the way many were expecting. I was lucky enough to be in the city the day before and could perceive the festival atmosphere. In listening to the speeches, in the majority of journalists and media operators, one heard brilliant — but not always well-founded — analyses and sometimes reckless predictions about the places where the pope would thunder most strongly against the worldliness of the Church. When the occasion took place, however, the pope made his mark above all with his gestures and with his person, simple and mild, yet strong and determined. Through his encounter with the sick and the poor, his desire to immerse himself in the wounds of human pain, without any sensational speeches, he revitalized Saint Francis and the most intimate and lively lesson of his existence.

I could see him from a very short distance when he went to the church of Santa Chiara, to venerate the mortal remains of the saint, to pray in the church dedicated to her and meet — in the chapel that houses the famous crucifix before which Francis lived an extraordinary inner experience — the community of the Poor Clares, heirs of "their" Mother. I experienced what televised images, even the best ones, cannot fully give: the intensity and brightness of his gaze, those eyes that strike and fascinate, his full and captivating smile, capable of capturing even the most skeptical person. Yes, the pope's whole person is Franciscan! And the content of the words addressed to the nuns was all Franciscan, even though there were no quotations from Francis or Clare. Because the pope invited them to contemplate Christ made flesh, immersed up to the neck, we could say, in human history, and to live fully the community dimension, welcoming each sister precisely as a sister, a person always loved, despite all the limitations that humanity carries with it. Isn't this Franciscan teaching? Didn't Francis and Clare live contemplating Christ made man? Wasn't every choice they made inspired by the desire to follow in his footsteps, to repeat — in their own existence — the ways chosen by Christ in the time of his dwelling among men? And is it not written as much in the *Rule* of Francis as in that of Clare, "Let each one manifest to the other with certainty his [her] needs, for if a mother nourishes and loves her carnal son, how much more thoughtfully one must love and nourish his [her] spiritual brother [sister]?"[9]

Speaking to priests, men and women religious, and laypeople engaged in pastoral work at the Cathedral of San Rufino, the pope summed up his speech in three fundamental verbs: to listen, to walk, to proclaim: listen to the Word of God, walk together (synod), proclaim to the outskirts (peripheries). This fully Franciscan program summarized the entire life of Francis, a man shaped by the Word, who walked with his brothers, always, and made Christ present in the peripheries of humanity. There are different types peripheries, and they are closer to us than we may think. "The outskirt which hurt me a great deal was to find children in middle class families who didn't know how to make the Sign of the Cross. But you see, this is an outskirt! And I ask you, here in this diocese, are there children who do not know how to make the Sign of the Cross? Think about it. These are true outskirts of existence where God is absent."

The pope insisted above all on the dimension of faith, essential for understanding Francis: faith and the Gospel. He asked young people not to be afraid to make definitive choices, swimming upstream against the culture of the provisional that rages today. "Here in Assisi, close to the Portiuncula, I seem to hear the voice of Saint Francis repeating: 'The Gospel, the Gospel!'" "Everyone who follows Christ," he said in his homily,

> receives true peace, the peace that Christ alone can give, a peace

which the world cannot give. Many people, when they think of Saint Francis, think of peace; very few people, however, go deeper. What is the peace which Francis received, experienced, and lived, and which he passes on to us? It is the peace of Christ, which is born of the greatest love of all, the love of the cross. It is the peace which the Risen Jesus gave to his disciples when he stood in their midst (cf. Jn 20:19–20). Franciscan peace is not something saccharine. Hardly! That is not the real Saint Francis! Nor is it a kind of pantheistic harmony with forces of the cosmos. ... That is not Franciscan either! It is not Franciscan, but a notion that some people have invented! The peace of Saint Francis is the peace of Christ, and it is found by those who "take up" their "yoke," namely, Christ's commandment: Love one another as I have loved you.

The pope is perfectly right in reaffirming that "the peace of Saint Francis is the peace of Christ" and that the idea of a "pantheistic harmony with forces of the cosmos" is not Franciscan. But we know the figure of Saint Francis is often distorted, with many contemporary interpretations attributing ideas and attitudes to him that are more the imaginings of modern people than choices actually made by the Saint of Assisi![10]

It was thus an experience enlightened and shaped by faith that changed his life, because faith either changes life or it is not faith! This is the portrait of Saint Francis that Pope Francis delivered on his first visit to Assisi. One could almost smile when someone tries to say that the pope, with his style of speaking and acting, tends to favor a horizontal and almost relativistic view of life, were it not for certain malicious points that can be perceived behind some analyses that appear banal, made to serve aims that are not at all naive. It is a faith, therefore, that changes life, that changes the criteria of value judgments by putting the poor at the center, those whom no one would like to have around, because Christ did so, to the point of identifying with them (Mt 25:31–46). This explains the sensitivity shown by Pope Francis toward migrants, the decision to go to Lampedusa, to pray at the U.S.-Mexico border. Yes, Francis puts before our eyes realities that we would like to forget, that perhaps even, in our misery, we would like to not see. Because the perennial temptation of Christians is to live not according the measure of the Gospel, but to make a Gospel according to our own measure.

AN INCLUSIVE VISION

A significant Franciscan "passage" of Pope Francis is undoubtedly found in the extraordinary encyclical on the "care for our common home." Francis expressly drew inspiration for it — even the title — from the *Canticle of the Sun*. In it he describes the saint as

> the example par excellence of care for the vulnerable and of an integral ecology lived out joyfully and authentically. He is the patron saint of all who study and work in the area of ecology, and he is also much loved by non-Christians. He was particularly concerned for God's creation and for the poor and outcast. He loved, and was deeply loved for his joy, his generous self-giving, his openheartedness. He was a mystic and a pilgrim who lived in simplicity and in wonderful harmony with God, with others, with nature, and with himself. He shows us just how inseparable the bond is between concern for nature, justice for the poor, commitment to society, and interior peace.[11]

The pope speaks opportunely of "integral ecology," affirming that poverty and austerity were not, for Saint Francis, "mere veneer of asceticism, but something much more radical: a refusal to turn reality into an object simply to be used and controlled" (ibid., n. 11).

Francis therefore lived in "wonderful harmony with God, with others, with nature, and with himself." In this way, the pope sketches out a complete and effective inclusive synthesis. I say inclusive because — as I have already mentioned — partial readings of the experience of Francis of Assisi, aimed at highlighting one aspect of his multifaceted personality to the detriment, if not in opposition to, the other, have often crossed and clashed. In this way, many have made their own Francis for their own use and consumption, without worrying too much if the portrait they created was supported by the sources. This is how we came to have a Francis for all seasons, from the vegetarian, to the pacifist, to the patriot, and so on. He is thus ceaselessly vivisected, gradually extrapolating different aspects of his personality and then absolutizing them until they became the whole of that experience, often forgetting the source from which everything sprang: his relationship with the God of Jesus Christ. This is not the reading of Pope Francis, who in Assisi, on the occasion of the World Day of Prayer for Peace ("Thirst for Peace. Religions and Cultures in Dialogue," September 20, 2016), reflected on the words of Jesus on the cross: "I am thirsty!" exclaimed Saint Francis "for love of the suffering Lord, he was not ashamed to cry out and grieve loudly. This same reality must be in our hearts as we contemplate Christ Crucified, he who thirsts for love."

Even our own approach to this pontificate, which shows an extraordinary overall coherence — I dare say almost an extraordinary Franciscan coherence — must not be partial.

The Choice to Be Among the Marginalized

Three unpublished lectures on Saint Francis of Assisi, which the renowned historian Raoul Manselli gave in Milan between November 25, 1981, and January 19, 1983, form the subject of a small volume with an introduction by Marco Bartoli recently published by Edizioni Biblioteca Francescana in the Series "Presence of Saint Francis." Manselli was in those years the undisputed point of reference of international Franciscanism. In 1980, he published a biography of Francis and a volume on the testimonies of the companions of the saint and also published a large series of essays in scientific journals and in proceedings of conferences.

In his work, he naturally analyzed the sources with the expertise of a historian, careful to sift through every detail in an attempt to reconstruct a historically valid profile of Saint Francis. He purposely renounced "the friezes and decorations of anecdotes that end up being only stylistic in nature."[1] Such an undertaking had already been attempted at the end of the nineteenth century by Paul Sabatier in his extraordinary biography, which was a gut punch to those who for centuries had adopted an apologetic approach to the Saint of Assisi. Sabatier was, however, also a poet and throughout long pages of his work, poetry seemed to triumph over history, and with it an image of the Saint that served the Christian vision of its author, which contrasted with Catholic apologetics. Unlike the French scholar, Manselli stuck much more firmly to the choice he made.

When his work was published, however, not everyone fully understood its importance. In 1981, an anonymous reviewer in the respected magazine *Frate Francesco* — to which Manselli had lent his collaboration on several occasions — said that "[Manselli's] research and his presentation of Saint Francis appear to us more historical and less theological, we would dare to say too historical and less theological."[2] He thereby demonstrated a blatant misunderstanding of the epistemological status of the matter.

For his own part, in an important 1983 essay, "St Francis, From Human Suffering to the Crucified Christ,"[3] Manselli had the opportunity to point out that the volume "was received by all with cordiality and sympathy, but of course also with some perplexity and, let's face it, misunderstandings. That a large part of both [perplexity and misunderstandings] refer to Francis's conversion and to the historical representation of his ideal, it is completely understandable, also because a historical evaluation of the personality of the saint derives from it." Manselli's reading was in fact strongly based on the first lines of Francis's *Testament*:

> The Lord gave me, Brother Francis, thus to begin doing penance in this way: for when I was in sin, it seemed too bitter for me to see lepers. And the Lord himself led me among them and *I showed mercy to them*. And when I left them, what had seemed bitter to me was turned into sweetness of soul and body. And afterwards I delayed a little and left the world. (*Test* 1–3: *FF* 110)

He pointed out with acuity that the "pauper" motif, the choice of poverty, was totally absent in Francis's summary of the initial moment of his conversion. "This means," he argued, "that the central moment of Francis's conversion was not focused on poverty, but … the passage from one human condition to another, the acceptance of one's own insertion into marginality, the entrance among the excluded. ... Poverty is a common characteristic of these excluded people, and a concomitant and inevitable fact. But poverty is not the decisive factor of conversion."[4]

It should be noted that it is only in recent decades that the writings of the man from Assisi have finally assumed that centrality proclaimed at the time by Sabatier with regard to the reconstruction of his human and religious life. Nevertheless, I do not know to what extent Sabatier himself remained faithful to this enlightened statement of principle. It is certain that, for much of the twentieth century, evidence of Francis of Assisi's Christian experience has been sought above all within the imposing hagiographic corpus about him, which is also a source of many thorny problems.

In his biography, Manselli applies the brilliant intuition of the Protestant historian, but instead assigns particular importance to Francis's writings, again theorizing on the principle enunciated by Sabatier. This choice took on greater force especially after Manselli's death, when the idea that those writings should constitute the filter, the criterion of discernment through which to judge the quality of the sources and the biographical material on the man from Assisi, finally came to the fore.

These cornerstones therefore constitute the strength of these conferences in Milan. In them, Manselli highlights the way in which "the problem of poverty had been experienced before Saint Francis" (Conference III), the story of "Saint Francis and his time" (Conference I), focusing also on the relationship between "Saint Francis and Brother Leo" (Conference II) through the analysis of the two texts the saint addressed to Brother Leo and which the latter — fortunately — jealously preserved, allowing them to reach us. Manselli studied the two documents carefully. After invoking "the help of a colleague in paleography" (most probably Professor Armando Petrucci, in those same years professor at the University of Rome "La Sapienza"), he went personally both to Assisi and Spoleto, where the two originals are kept. The conclusion that the scholars agreed upon "is that the two documents attributed to Francis are undoubtedly authentic."[5] This conclusion was later confirmed by Attilio Bartoli Langeli, who in more recent decades had the opportunity to examine both texts in depth.[6]

Studying the letter kept in Spoleto, Manselli observed that the first lines "are in beautiful script, they are very calligraphic, but as we proceed down the lines, the writing becomes more and more uncertain, the hand less sure."[7] Finally, he admitted,

> I must confide to you that, while I wracked my brain, the intuition came to my wife, who was sick for many months. She told me, "Don't you see? It's like when I was writing from the hospital: my first two or three lines were fine, but then as I had to go further, I was so weak that the writing was lost to me, it fell apart, so to speak, in my hands." This means that we are dealing with a letter from Francis's last days, when his eyes and strength were progressively abandoning him.[8]

After the death of the professor, I met his wife, Iris, and I was touched as I thought about them together, at her husband's desk, staring at the photocopies of the documents whose secrets they tried to penetrate. I imagine them now, and I trust that they are together again, admiring Saint Francis in the splendor of heavenly glory.

The Man Who Became Prayer

In the short text in prose that precedes the flow of the verses in *Francesco. Canto di una creatura* ("Francis. Song of a Creature of God" [2007]), Alda Merini affirms that "our soul is sad, even to the point of death, because man is afraid, afraid to believe." However, this is not the only fear that we too often allow ourselves to be sucked into. Even the fear of making mistakes, and therefore of submitting to the judgment of others, often surrounds us to the point of almost suffocating us. It is interesting, in this regard, to reread what the poetess confided to Francesco Nati in an interview of January 5, 2008, a few months after the publication of her book. According to Merini, "Perhaps neither Manganelli nor Quasimodo nor Sereni, perhaps not even Turoldo," had "sensed the aroma of divine providence, of the Great Master. They were afraid of making mistakes, even talking, renouncing this general stripping away of all the trappings, to appear naked and perfect as God made us. Why cover ourselves with cloaks? We are the most beautiful divine work, a work that we will never stop paying back."

Not Francis! He had stripped himself of everything that could adorn the old man, and in his nakedness showed the beauty of divine glory. Again in that interview, to Nati's question "What do you see in Saint Francis?" Merini answered that she understood in the brother of Assisi's Christian experience the beauty of "the total renunciation of the cares of men and above all the beauty of small things, the daily discovery of life, the fact of feeling alive even after being martyred, violated, and yet still smiling, still wondering why, despite everything, you are happy." Her reading clearly connected with the poet's life story, arising several times from the rubble, after repeated falls that led her to long stretches in various psychiatric hospitals.

Francesco is a poetic monologue in which Alda Merini offers her understanding of the saint of Assisi. The man of God speaks in a sequence that doesn't have its own apparent internal coherence. It is rather a succession of instants, each of high stylistic validity, in which the same interweaving of two events appears: that of Francis and that of Alda Merini. The young man from Assisi, rich and ultimately spoiled, was not understood by his parents, especially by his father, who would have liked to direct his son's path in his own way. Alda, for her part, after attending vocational school, had to interrupt her studies for family reasons, a fact that produced a break that was difficult to repair in her psychology. In both cases the family situation — even if for different reasons — conditioned the existence of both people. I believe, therefore, that there are still autobiographical traces in the many verses (here I will address only a few) that Merini dedicates to the controversial relationship between Francis and his father, in an attempt to penetrate the reasons for a fatherly love incapable of comprehension and the harshness of a son — as indeed it was — toward his father:

> My father, whom I loved so much, / was dressed in pure lies. / And he rejoiced only / when I enjoyed those goods / to feed my vices. But how can I understand a father / who in the flesh of a son / saw his own future? How I disappointed him, / how he cried for me / and I cry with Ser Bernardone / over everything we left together, / our mutual deceptions. But is it right, Lord, to forget / he who in his own way loved us / covering us with mon-

ey / and sumptuous clothes? / It is the misery of a parent / who does not understand / that a child belongs to God. / But a man like my father, / who was afraid of death, / how could he understand? / Money is an excuse / to defend oneself from death, / a mask under which man hides / not to show that he is an angel, / a sad and troubled angel. / I wanted to be naked, / I wanted to be only soul. And again: How many mistakes do fathers make / by covering with gems / their children who want poverty and work / and familiarity with God.

The saint, stripped of all things, thus became the friend of God, following in the footsteps of he who was from the beginning, who spoke and all things were created, and who chose to strip and be stripped of all things in order to lead man back to the sublimity of his vocation. Made a friend of God, Francis is therefore capable of seeing men and things with the eyes of God. "What man finds useless, / the smallest things, the most insignificant silences, / God finds extremely precious. / Therefore I will save every blade of grass, therefore the forgotten creatures / will become my creatures: / the marginalized, the crippled, / those whom man / does not want to receive in his heart, / but whom death embraces, / this sister whom I love above all else."

Immersed in the mystery, he was not so much a man who prayed — Thomas of Celano said of Francis — but who became prayer (*non tam orans quam oratio factus*). A prayer that, according to Merini, "is nothing: / it is a tomb that must be devastated, / devastated to the point of spasm, / to bring forth the sole Word, / the true Word of God." The Word that alone can tell the truth of all things, that alone is capable of making all creatures into a single symphonic hymn of praise to God and makes man mad for his Lord:

> And I am mad, / mad as you, Lord, / mad with love. I have become the bridge between your birth / and your resurrection. / Walk over me, / trample on Francis / to reach Calvary.

The person of the saint, his humanity, thus becomes almost a personification of the existence of the Son of God, in a *christomimesis* that in the existence of one reflects and rereads that of the other.

And then there is Clare, "who could have been / the gymnasium of my love, / and instead became / the inspiring muse / of the dream of God." In the same interview given to Francesco Nati, Merini said that Clare "was a great love of Francis, like that of Joseph for Our Lady, the guardian of a heart. Both guarded the heart of the woman. It was magnificent: They did not protect the flesh of the woman, but the heart, that heart which was torn from so many women by violence." Here too, what an extraordinary interweaving of lives! "O woman, angelic and sublime, / how can I not become a great poet / singing your sublime weariness?" "We are two torches of love for God, / but we have discovered, divine companion, / that if our body / is a prison with a thousand bars, / afterwards the avalanche of the sky opens up."

Alda Merini's Francis is capable of transmitting the restlessness of faith and for this reason I feel like proposing it again today. Because only a restless faith, said Cardinal Carlo Maria Martini, can be a thinking faith!

Conclusion

As I mentioned at the beginning of these pages, Brother Masseo, amazed at Francis's ability to fascinate, who attracted whole crowds to himself, was not afraid to remind him that he was not "a man fair of body" (*Flor* 10: *FF* 1838). Was a sort of law of contrasts influencing the lost Masseo, who was not yet completely free from worldly categories? Perhaps so, especially if we take into account that he was physically attractive, something that must have furnished him with followers and favors in the world. Whereas now he was facing a different reality, in which the one followed and adored was a man completely devoid of those qualities otherwise so appreciated by people. And it was precisely this that he could not understand, because he himself still experienced how much appearance was able to obscure everything else.

Francis chose Masseo as his companion on the way to

> the province of France. And coming one day to a village and being very hungry, they went, according to the Rule, begging bread for the love of God; and Saint Francis went through one street

and Friar Masseo through another. But because Saint Francis was a man too despicable and small of body, and was esteemed a vile mendicant therefore by those who knew him not, he got only some mouthfuls and fragments of dry bread; whereas to Friar Masseo, because he was tall and beautiful of body, were given good pieces and large and in plenty and fresh cut from the loaf.[1]

However, Francis's humanity was full of God, which ended up overturning every normal standard of value and judgment. The whole world therefore followed him.

It may seem surprising — and maybe it is — that after refusing an anecdotal and devotional reading of Francis of Assisi and his life experience, I opened and closed this book with pages of the *Little Flowers* in which the protagonists are Saint Francis and Brother Masseo. If I have chosen these pages, however, it is because, beyond their evergreen appeal, they help us to understand — perhaps better than many others — that human logic does not always prevail and that the Gospel also has its reasons, which reason does not have. Francis, who for the first twenty-four years of his existence had lived oblivious to God, making himself the center of the world, made of himself a total gift to God and to his brothers and sisters in the twenty years that remained to him to live. And he did so with such intensity that those who came into contact with him ended up seriously questioning their relationship with the Lord and their experience of faith.

Only if it is meaningful, only if it really changed our lives, can our experience of faith help others to find the way to God. Therefore, reading the story of Francis and meditating on it will be of no use if it does not help us to become "better Christians" (*Lmin* 5: *FF* 234). For what "great shame" it would be for us, if "the saints have completed their works" and if we should wish to receive "their glory and honor simply for telling about them" (*Adm* VI, 3: *FF* 155).

Notes

INTRODUCTION
1. *Flo* 10.

2. Exceptions are: "Saint Francis in Rieti," unpublished, and "An Inclusive Vision," in *Credere Oggi* 37 (March, 2017) n. 219, pp. 173–186.

FROM HUMAN SUFFERING TO THE CRUCIFIED CHRIST
1. R. Manselli, *San Francesco d'Assisi, Editio maior*, San Paolo, Cinisello Balsamo 2002, p. 131.

CAN'T YOU SEE MY HOUSE IS COLLAPSING?
1. Cf. S. Gieben, "Das Tafelkreuz von S. Damiano in der Geschichte. Mit einem ikonographischen Anhang," in *Collectanea Franciscana* 71 (2001), pp. 47–63.

2. *3Comp* 13: *FF* 1411.

3. Cf. ibid., pp. 61–62.

4. *Fonti clariane*, no. 2161–2162.

5. In *Collectanea Franciscana* 84 (2014), p. 395.

HOW WHAT WAS BITTER BECAME SWEET
1. R. Manselli, *San Francesco dal dolore degli uomini al Cristo crocifisso, in Id., Francesco e i suoi compagni* (Bibliotheca seraphico-capuccina, 46), Rome 1995, p. 187.

2. *Lmin* 9–11: *FF* 235.

EXCESS IS THEFT
1. Homily VI, 7; text from *Povertà e ricchezza nel cristianesimo primitivo*, ed. M.G. Mara, Rome 1980, p. 172.

2. *Gaudium et Spes*, n. 69.

3. *Rnb* IX, 4–8: *FF* 31, emphasis added.

FRANCIS, PEACE, AND ARMS
1. Cf. S. Migliore, *Mistica povertà. Riscritture francescane tra '800 e '900* (Biblio-

teca seraphico-capuccina, 64), Rome 2001.

2. *Lmin* 2–7: *FF* 234.

3. Cf. *Anper* 19: *FF* 1509; *3Comp* 26: *FF* 1428.

4. Cf. Salimbene de Adam, *Cronica*, ed. G. Scalia (Corpus christianorum. Continuatio Mediaevalis, 125), Turnholti 1998, p. 107.

5. Cf. P. Evangelisti, *Fidenzio da Padova e la letteratura crociato-missionaria minoritica. Strategie e modelli francescani per il dominio (XIII–XIV sec.)* (Istituto Italiano per gli Studi Storici in Napoli, 43) Bologna 2000.

WHEN FRANCIS PREDICTED THE EARTHQUAKE

1. *Eccleston* 166–67: *FF* 2460.

2. Cf. J.-G. Bougerol, *La teorizzazione dell'esperienza di S. Francesco negli autori francescani pre-bonaventuriani*, in *Lettura biblico-teologica delle fonti francescane*, a cura di G. Cardaropoli e M. Conti, Rome 1979, pp. 257–260.

3. J. D. Rasolofoarimanana, *Jean de La Rochelle et Anonime. Trois sermons* de Sanctis *sur saint François d'Assise dans le ms. Clm 7776*, in *Frate Francesco* 67 (2001), p. 63, rr. 60–62.

4. Cf. I. Brady, *Saint Bonaventure's Sermons on St. Francis*, in *Franziskanische Studien* 58 (1976), pp. 129–141.

5. *FF* 2252.

THE POOR KING

1. *LOrd* 26–29: *FF* 221.

LISTEN, POOR LADIES

1. G. Salvadori, *Lettere I (1878–1906)*, ed. N. Vian, Rome 1976, pp. 353–354.

2. p. 18.

3. pp. 17–18.

SAINT FRANCIS IN RIETI

1. Cf. A. Sacchetti Sassetti, *Anecdota Franciscana Reatina*, Potenza 1926, pp. 40–44.

2. Cf. ibid., pp. 38–40, 44–47.

THE LITTLE PLANT OF BROTHER FRANCIS
1. *1Cel* 116: *FF* 524.

BEWARE OF THE MAN, NOT THE WOLF
1. *FF* 2251.

2. Primo Mazzolari, *Incontro al lupo. Con "S. Francesco uomo libero,"* ed. L. G. Viale, Mantua 1970, pp. 29–30.

BLAME THE TOWER OF BABEL
1. Angelus, Sunday, September 6, 2015.
2. *Jordan* 27: *FF* 2354.

SAINT FRANCIS, THE MOST ITALIAN OF SAINTS
1. Cf. V. Gioberti, *Del primato morale e civile degli italiani*. First edition of Lausanne based on the second Belgian, edition t. II, Lausanne 1846, pp. 360–-361.

2. In Raffaele da Paterno, *Omaggio del mondo cattolico a San Francesco d'Assisi nella ricorrenza del VII Centenario dalla nascita 1882* VI–VII. *Omaggio delle arti, delle lettere e della carità a S. Francesco*, Napoli 1886, p. 98.

3. The entire article is reported by S. Franchini, *Sugli esordi della Società internazionale di studi francescani fondata da Paul Sabatier* (Medioevo francescano. Opuscoli, 1), S. Maria degli Angeli 2002, pp. 78–79, n. 109.

4. In S. Migliore, *Mistica povertà. Riscritture francescane tra Otto e Novecento*, Rome 2001, pp. 328–329.

AN INCLUSIVE VISION: SAINT FRANCIS ACCORDING TO POPE FRANCIS
1. In this brief study I will obviously not be able to take into account all the occasions on which the pope referred to Saint Francis of Assisi. I shall therefore limit myself to offering an overall view by referring to what I consider his most significant speeches.

2. Cf. *Test* 1–3 (*FF* 110). On the importance of this passage in relation to the definition of the content of the choice made by Francis, see, among others, R. Manselli, *San Francesco d'Assisi*, pp. 106–113; Id., *San Francesco dal dolore degli uomini al Cristo crocifisso*; Miccoli, *La proposta cristiana di Francesco d'Assisi*, in Id., *Francesco d'Assisi. Realtà e memoria di un'esperienza cristiana* (Einaudi Paperbacks, 217), Torino 1991, pp. 52–53. Manselli's essays were originally published in 1980 and 1983;

Miccoli's in 1983.

3. R. Manselli, *San Francesco*, p. 109.

4. Regarding Francis's *Testament*, other than K. Esser, *Das Testament des heiligen Franziskus von Assisi*, Munster in W. 1949, see P. Maranesi, *L'eredità di frate Francesco. Lettura storico-critica del Testamento* (Studi e ricerche, s.n.), S. Maria degli Angeli-Assisi 2009. I also suggest the critical review of L. Lehmann, *Studi sul Testamento di Francesco d'Assisi a partire dall'edizione di Kajetan Esser del 1949*, in *Frate Francesco* 80 (2014), pp. 331–374.

5. G. Miccoli, *Un'esperienza cristiana tra Vangelo e I stituzione*, in *Dalla "Sequela Christi" all'apologia della povertà*. Atti del XVIII Convegno internazionale, 18–20 Ottobre 1990, Spoleto 1992, p. 20.

6. The reading of R. Manselli, *San Francesco dal dolore degli uomini al Cristo crocifisso*, is always stimulating in this regard.

7. In *Considerations on the Stigmata* III it is said in fact that Brother Leo, while he was once with Francis on La Verna, now approaching the feast of the Exaltation of the Cross (September 14), went to the place and time set for prayer; seeing that Francis did not respond, in contravention of the order, he set out to search for him, until he heard his voice and then saw him in prayer "with his face and hands raised to heaven, and in fervor of spirit so said: 'Who are you, my sweetest God? What am I, the most vile vermin and useless servant of thine?'" (*FF* 1915). On the *Considerations on the Stigmata*, which in many manuscripts immediately follow the text of the little flowers, I refer you to F. Lapièrre, *La vida a la luz de la pasión de san Francisco. Análisis de un itinerario spiritual en la fuente "La consideración sobre las llagas" divulgada en los "Fioretti,"* in *Un aporte a la historia de la cultura de los siglos XVII–XX*. II Simposio sobre Bibliotecas y Archivos del área franciscana en América España y Portugal. Buenos Aires, 26–28 de Agosto 2004. Coordinatores J. Brunader C. A. Lértora Mendoza, Buenos Aires 2005, pp. 305–322.

8. Pope Francis expressly affirms that he considers Saint Francis as "his" saint. Take for example what he says in his greeting (November 2016) to the Patriarch of Moscow Kirill, on the seventieth birthday of the head of the Russian Orthodox Church. On this occasion Pope Francis donated to Kirill (the press office of the Patriarchate of Moscow made it known by reporting the message of good wishes of the pontiff) some relics of Saint Francis of Assisi, to thank him for the gift in turn received from part of the relics of Saint Seraphim of Sarov: "I am happy," said the pope on the occasion, "to offer a part of the relics of Saint Francis of Assisi, my heavenly protector."

9. For Francis, cf. *Rb* VI, 8 (*FF* 91; but see already *Rnb* IX, 10–11: *FF* 32); for Clare, cf. *RsC* VIII, 15–16 (*FF* 2798). Clare inserts these statements in the section in which she deals with sick sisters; and it is precisely in her attention to the sick sisters that the evangelical and Franciscan spirit of Clare is fully manifested: cf. also *RsC* V, 3 (*FF* 2783), where it is stated that in the infirmary, "for the relief and service of the sick," it is "always allowed for the sisters" to "speak with discretion." The rule of silence was therefore not taken into account. Neither does Clare mention the recommendation in the *Constitutions* of Ugolino (cf. n. 8) and in the *Form of Life* of Innocent IV (cf. n. 4), texts which were also for her a point of comparison, which asked, where possible, to establish a separate dwelling for the sick, in order to safeguard, in this way, "the order and quiet of the others."

10. As has rightly been pointed out, "The public and contemporary uses of the figure of the Saint today often tend to indicate Francis's attitude toward peace as the most important and characteristic aspect of his Christian experience, while neglecting to understand it as a natural consequence of his evangelical conception. Abstracted from the context from which it takes its meaning and actualized, this attitude takes on mythical and ideal contours, ending up presenting itself as an invention of memory rather than as a witness to history" (S. Migliore, San Francesco e lo "spirito di Assisi," in *Convivium Assisiense* 9 (2007), pp. 54–55). And again: "The excessive insistence on the pacifist and defenseless dimension of Francis of Assisi — outside, above all, the context of *imitatio Christi* which inspired it — implies the risk of great misrepresentations" (ibid., p. 55). Much profit can be made from reading a book by the same author: S. Migliore, *Mistica povertà. Riscritture francescane tra Otto e Novecento*.

11. *Laudato si'*, n. 10.

THE CHOICE TO BE AMONG THE MARGINALIZED

1. R. Manselli, *San Francesco* (Biblioteca di cultura, 182), Rome 1980, p. 5

2. In *Frate Francesco* 48 (1981), pp. 51–52.

3. *San Francesco dal dolore degli uomini al Cristo crocifisso*, p. 183, note 1.

4. R. Manselli, *San Francesco d'Assisi. Editio maior* (Tempi e figure, 41), Cinisello Balsamo 2002, pp. 109–110.

5. R. Manselli, *Tre conferenze inedite*, p. 47.

6. Cf. A. Bartoli Langeli, *Gli scritti da Francesco: l'autografia di un "illtteratus,"* in *Frate Francesco d'Assisi. Atti del XXI Convegno internazionale. Assisi, 14–16 Ottobre 1993*, Spoleto 1994, pp. 101–159; Id., *Gli autografi di frate Francesco e di frate*

Leone (Autographa Medii Aevi, 5), Turnout 2000.
 7. R. Manselli, *Tre conferenze inedite*, p. 62.
 8. Ibid.

CONCLUSION
 1. *Flo* 13: *FF* 1841.